HOW TO PLAY THE
CHESS OPENINGS

HOW TO PLAY THE CHESS OPENINGS

by

Eugene A. Znosko-Borovsky

ENGLISH VERSION

by

G. E. SMITH, B.A.

Chess Editor of *The Field* and translator of
Dr. Tarrasch's *Das Schachspiel,*

and

W. M. DASH, B.A.

DOVER PUBLICATIONS, INC.
NEW YORK

CONTENTS

CONTENTS—*continued*

INTRODUCTION

I have been so teased—although in a friendly way—on the title of my last brochure, *How Not to Play Chess*,* that I am now attempting to teach "How to Play Chess." Nevertheless, I persist in my attitude and I insist on beginning with the beginning, on opening with the Opening. It is true that we often see manuals which begin with the End-Game. I have good reasons for not following their example, for the Opening is the most important phase of the game and certainly cannot be avoided. Error in the Opening is irremediable and gives one the discouraging feeling of having not even had a game. Moreover, it is in the openings that some manuals overwhelm one with variations, sub-variations, letters, figures, and all sorts of parentheses, in which one is hopelessly lost without learning anything.

Even if one manages to learn by heart—and not to confuse—all these variations, one is in no less of a difficulty when having to use one's own imagination. As a result of playing the openings automatically and relying on memory instead of on an understanding of the game, one does not know how to refute an inferior move, simply because it is not to be found in the books. The dogmatism of the books becomes a despotism; and amateurs become accustomed to regarding the moves made by such and such a master or indicated by such and such a book as obligatory moves, so that any diversion is prejudged as dangerous or bad.

To my way of thinking, this point of view is totally false. In this search for a truth—a little truth of the chessboard but, nevertheless, a truth—represented by the theory of the openings, each one should have a creative part. Each move in the openings is merely an attempt to solve such or such a problem and should expect to be refuted, each variation requires to be revised or strengthened. There are only a very few points in the theory of the openings which may be considered as fixed, absolutely and beyond appeal. And every day amateurs of no great strength discover the refutations of some well-established variations.

* (Dover reprint.)

Without, however, demanding that every "tyro" should become an explorer instead of travelling on a conducted tour, I insist on this point—that everyone should be in a position to discover a good move (if not the best) and the way, in no matter what position, to reply to any innovation. It is then not simply on memory but, above all, on intelligence that one should rely to achieve this result and it is not of such importance to *learn* variations as to *understand* their meaning. One must become imbued with the spirit of an opening and play it in the appropriate style. Besides the general principles common to all the openings, one must know and understand the characteristics of each. The choice of an opening will frequently depend upon the player's mood at the moment. One does not choose a Caro-Kann if one feels aggressive, and one must not venture upon a gambit if one does not feel very lively.

It is on these lines that this book is conceived. I shall not multiply variations; those I give are there only as examples. On the other hand, I do emphasise well-known traps, or mistakes frequently made by amateurs, in order to save my readers from the disappointment of losing through an elementary blunder. I have maintained throughout a simple method of presentation in order not to confuse beginners and also to save them unnecessary labour which might cause that distaste for the study and even the playing of the game that is so often experienced after heavy reading of too erudite chess manuals.

The various questions that are propounded to the reader in the course of this book have no other aim than to stimulate his imagination and to give him a foretaste of what he will have to do in actual play. The answers will be found at the end of the book.

In conclusion, I thank in advance those readers who may favour me with their suggestions regarding the book itself or my method. These suggestions I will bear in mind in any further editions of this book.

May this little book receive from the numerous lovers of our wonderful game that kindly welcome which they have given to my previous works.

EUGENE ZNOSKO-BOROVSKY.

A LITTLE HISTORY

"Chess is a game of understanding and not of memory."
This maxim, with which I opened my brochure, *How
Not to Play Chess*, has met with universal approval,
and there is no reason for not applying it to the
study of the openings ! It is not, then, by memorising
variations that we shall become proficient in playing openings, but by understanding their meaning, their purpose,
and the general ideas and principles which are their founda-
tion. However, we must not on this account ignore the
acquisitions of the past ; certain ideas, accumulated during
the centuries, are still as valuable to-day as ever before.

It is always a good thing to survey the past, and in a
treatise on chess, however small, the historical side has its
importance. But let us be brief and not lose touch with
essentials. Making a rapid survey of this history, and
extracting from it the underlying principles which governed
the treatment of the openings at various times, we are not
a little surprised to realise that these principles do not
contradict one another but, on the contrary, that each new
principle links on to the older ones, completes them, widens
the knowledge possessed before, and in close relation with
it, helps forward the treatment of the openings.

There is no name more worthy to head a work on chess
than that of Morphy, who embodies the very spirit of the
game ; and although he was no theoretician, we think of
him when discussing the theory of the openings. For if
others have taken a more prominent part in the elaboration
of the first principles concerning the development of the
pieces, we are indebted to him for a brilliant demonstration
of them. His genius enabled him to realise clearly what
others could but vaguely discern. Morphy's style was much
in advance of the theory of his day, and he dominated all
his contemporaries not only by his brilliant combinations,
but also—and above all—by his characteristic way of dealing
with the openings.

Of course there was then no coherent theory as we

understand it now. There were then only scattered and isolated principles which helped the player in the opening. We can condense them all into a single one of first-rate importance, which was stated for the first time, apparently, by that great French player, de La Bourdonnais, and which still holds good to-day. We are speaking here of the necessity of developing the pieces as quickly as possible at the beginning of a game. Accordingly we begin with the two centre pawns, then we bring out the pieces one by one, we castle, etc., in preference to moving the same piece several times : but all to be done as rapidly as possible.

RULE I.   RAPID DEVELOPMENT OF THE PIECES.

Formulated thus, the marked difference between this principle and the manner of treating the openings before Morphy's time is not quite evident. Even the fantastic gambits of the past were played with the object of hindering the enemy development. Nevertheless, the difference does exist. For in a gambit, where the purpose is an immediate attack, the development of the majority of the pieces is often neglected, for the player is determined to force checkmate with only two or three pieces in play. Morphy held the opposite view : he was always thinking, alike in attack and defence, of the development of all his pieces, so that he was always ahead of his opponent in concentrating larger forces on the most important part of the board. In these circumstances, he needed no brilliant combinations to give him victory : or, at least, their creation was greatly simplified on this account.

Little by little others followed his example : pieces were brought out just for the sake of rapid development, but without any definite object, while they were sometimes posted more by luck than by judgment. The general principle, with which all development must comply, had yet to be discovered.

RULE 2.   OCCUPATION OF THE CENTRE.

Thanks to Steinitz, a new scheme came into being to supplement Morphy's ideas and to establish laws for the treatment of the openings. It was no longer a question of scattered rules, for a modern school was formed which gradually superseded the so-called classical school.

The precepts of this new school, based on quasi-scientific data, referred to the game as a whole, and the revolution in ideas, when applied to the openings, completely changed the character of them. The Gambits and the Giuoco Piano were replaced by the Ruy Lopez, the Queen's Pawn Game, the French Defence, etc. To illustrate the important position occupied by these openings, it is enough to recall that of over 200 games given in Dr. Tarrasch's famous book, *Die moderne Schachpartie*, in barely 40 were the older openings played. The remainder were the so-called modern openings.

Everybody is well aware now of the principles of the new school, for the whole game is steeped in them. But though its doctrines—the first real doctrines of chess—were brought to such perfection by experts like Tarrasch, Rubinstein and Schlechter, they were at first far from satisfactory. Their strangeness sometimes provoked an opposition which seems to us quite a natural one. Did not their inventor, the great Steinitz, himself play K—K2 in the opening of a game ? Did he never, as White, play his Knight to KR3 or defend a gambit by making a sortie with his Queen to KB3 ? But all this is recorded in history. Nowadays, without even thinking about the modern school—so deeply are its ideas rooted in our minds—we are acquainted with its principles right from the importance of the centre and of open lines and the need of occupying them with the appropriate pieces down to the ideas of strong and weak squares, of isolated and doubled pawns, etc. One of these principles, that no pawn advance should be made without very good reason, has often been criticised—it is even now accused of robbing the game of its life and brilliance. For Steinitz, the pawns formed the *skeleton* of the game, and he never went so far as to declare, as did that first positional player, Philidor, that the pawns are the *soul* of the game of chess.

As regards the opening, then, the most important principle is the occupation of the centre. From it all others depend—it must govern the whole of our tactics. The centre is the very basis of the game.

It is clear now what is meant by the idea of developing the pieces. The legacy of the 19th century to us is that great truth : "Develop the pieces as rapidly as possible *in order to occupy the centre.*"

RULE 3.   THE GENERAL PLAN.

The 20th century, although still young, has not been behindhand in bringing forward its own scientific contribution and for this we are indebted to Capablanca. Like Morphy, a practical player, first and foremost, he is no theoretician, but the upheaval he has made in the theory of the openings and in the game generally can be compared, in its importance and fruitfulness, to the revolution brought about by Steinitz.

In his book, *Die neuen Ideen im Schachspiel*, Réti writes about him at length and recounts how, in a game he (Réti) played in consultation with Capablanca, the latter refused to make a plausible move—the best according to classical tradition—and made instead another of which Réti had not even dreamt, so unnatural was it. It involved the moving of an already developed piece a second time against all the classical principles of good development.

Réti's instance is not very convincing, for, as it turned out, Capablanca had only taken advantage of a tactical possibility offered him. But Réti was quite right in saying that Capablanca had initiated a new method of treating the openings, and this new formula, called by its followers " dynamic," has given rise to all the modern ideas of mobility.

Capablanca did not deny the principles of Morphy and of the new school, but submitted them to the test of a general plan, of a game of massed pieces, of a game directed towards a single goal from its very first moves. It is not sufficient to bring out the pieces rapidly, to group them round the centre, or to place them on central squares. The essential is to develop them in accordance with a general plan. There are on the board good squares—strong squares—and they must be occupied : but most important of all, the value of a square depends on the correlation of the pieces. It is not enough, therefore, to occupy a strong square as such (because if this were so, there would be an end of openings for they would be played always in the same way), but we must occupy a square which becomes important owing to the relative position of the pieces.

Thus we may delay bringing a piece into play so that we may post it, later, on a really important square where it will actively co-operate with the other pieces. Henceforth, it is action which counts ; it is the mobility of the pieces which is important, because by it the value of a square is changed. A square may be strong without necessarily offering scope for the action of pieces occupying it. In the positional game one is content with the possession of strong squares and the game progresses in bounds, so to speak, from one strong position to another, at the same time leaving no weaknesses. Nowadays, on the other hand, the value of a post is subordinated to the degree of mobility and the scope it offers to the pieces.

The ultra-modern "dynamic" game succeeds the "static" positional game.

The importance of this new principle is already evident. The rapid development (Morphy) and the occupation of the centre (Steinitz) appear to us as purely mechanical beside this new law, which introduces the general idea, the idea present right from the opening.

Thus Alekhine affirmed that there was no reason for dividing the game into the opening, the middle game and the end-game, for a game of chess is a complete thing, bound by the same rules at each stage of its duration and having in view a single object. The unity of the game, essential for logical play and for the development of chess ideas, was discovered.

This gave birth to another tendency characterised by the refusal, for a time, of immediate conflict, by the desire of postponing a premature hand-to-hand combat. This tendency, which is closely connected to Capablanca's "dynamic" idea, has been, just as was Steinitz's positional game, the target for severe criticism on the part of lovers of the brilliant game, the game of combinations, for, according to them, it shows in the players a fear of the open struggle and an unconfessed desire for a peaceful draw.

However, all the regular openings, in which the centre is controlled as quickly as possible, often lead to rapid exchanges which simplify the game and lessen the chances of victory. Sometimes even the occupation of the centre becomes either impossible or valueless. So it appeared to be wiser to avoid immediate contact of the pieces in the early stages of the game and to post them circumspectly on central squares where they could not be exchanged and from which they could not be driven away.

RULE 4. CONTROL OF THE CENTRE.

This brings us to a new idea which gives a wider meaning to the occupation of the centre. Occupation of the centre no longer means merely placing our pieces there but keeping the centre under control so that our opponent is not allowed to occupy it, while we reserve for ourselves the opportunity to do so efficaciously at a given moment. What is true for the centre is also true for any other squares.

The mechanical game of the past gives way to the game of relative values : both squares and pieces vary in importance. Everything is set in motion and the materialistic side of the game is subordinated to ideas. An unchanging table of values for the pieces, *e. g.* Queen=10, Rook=5, etc., has no longer any meaning. It is no longer a question of posting the strongest pieces rapidly on the strongest squares, but of keeping those squares under control and of manœuvring the pieces accordingly. It is the same with moves ; a move is weak if it does not form part of a line of play ; a move which is apparently weak may prove strong if it leads up to a series of manœuvres and is justified by the result. Thus chess loses any mechanical aspect ; the mind dominates it ; the game of understanding has become a game of intellect expressing itself as a work of art.

It is with the idea of initiating you into this new art that I am going to explain the various openings to you. For do not they, like the rudiments of music or the first lessons in drawing, present the most difficulty ?

CLASSIFICATION OF THE OPENINGS

The idea of the centre, as we have seen in the foregoing explanation, is at the base of all the openings. Its occupation is of primary importance at the beginning of a game. The reasons for this are already well known and, without lingering for long over this matter, we will just briefly recall them to mind.

The centre is important because every piece is stronger the nearer it is to it. A Knight in the corner of a board has only two moves at its disposal, while in the centre it has eight. Further, the central squares are most important because they are equidistant from all corners of the board, so that in commanding the centre, the whole board is also commanded ; at an opportune moment, any piece, posted at the centre, can be easily brought into attack or defence, while, if placed in the corners, it will lose considerable time in crossing the board. It may happen that in the course of a game one wing becomes the theatre of operations and consequently more important than the centre. In the opening, however, the centre is always more important, because the game has taken no definite direction, and one must be prepared for action from all sides at any time.

However, this occupation of the centre assumes a different character with each opening. If you choose an ultra-modern opening, you make use of the ultra-modern ideas on the observation of the centre. In this case you will put out of your mind all ideas of an immediate and tentative occupation of the centre. Similarly if you play an open game, you will be inspired by the classical ideas of the theory of the openings, and you must not introduce methods which are far removed from them. It is a question of style as much as of logic.

Above all, you must grasp the general idea of an opening in order to be able to use it freely afterwards and to find moves which are in accordance with it. On the basis of the

fundamental ideas of the various openings we can classify
the openings into four groups :—

1. The Open Game (1. P—K4, P—K4). The establishment of a King-centre* by both White and Black.

2. The Close Game (1. P—Q4, P—Q4). The establishment of a Queen-centre* by both White and Black.

3. The Half-Open Game (1. P—K4, Black making any
move other than 1. .... P—K4). The establishment by
Black of a Queen-centre in opposition to White's King-
centre.

4. The Modern Openings ((a) 1. P—Q4, Black making any
move other than 1. .... P—Q4 ; (b) White makes any move
other than 1. P—K4 or 1. P—Q4). In the first case Black
refuses the immediate occupation of the centre in reply to
White's establishment of a Queen-centre ; in the second
both players abstain from occupying the centre.

It must not be thought that all other moves are bad and
lead to an unavoidable loss. The most ridiculous moves
can be made without necessarily bringing about defeat. In
a consultation game, that great master Tchigorin played
1. P—QR4 and 2. P—R5—and even then won the game.
But that is an exception, and it is preferable at first to follow
the natural course of the openings so that later on one may
allow oneself to make experiments.

In the analysis of each separate group, we shall attempt
to find in it the directive ideas and the line of play they
involve, and when we pass on to the study of each opening
in a group, we shall be able to distinguish its characteristics.
When engaged in a game, the player will do just the
opposite. The idea that he wants to develop will dictate
to him the opening to choose.

---

* As the author frequently uses the terms "King-centre" and
"Queen-centre," an explanation of them will, perhaps, not be
out of place. By the former he means a central pawn formation
containing at least a pawn at K4, while in the latter the central
pawn formation contains at least a pawn at Q4.

FIRST GROUP

OPEN GAMES
(1. P—K4, P—K4)

If each opening is based upon an idea peculiar to itself, what is then the idea underlying the open games, determining their characteristics and distinguishing them from other opening systems ?

This idea is essentially the rapid occupation of the centre by the pawns and the pieces. The word centre is here applied primarily to the four squares, Q4 and K4 on either side (the little centre) and, in a secondary sense, to the sixteen central squares (the enlarged centre). It goes without saying that in this system one must follow Morphy's principle : a rapid development of the pieces and their grouping around the centre and on the central lines.

CENTRE GAME
(1. P—K4, P—K4 ; 2. P—Q4)

Let us attempt first of all the immediate occupation of the little centre and after playing the King's pawn two squares, let us advance the Queen's pawn to Q4 without any preparation and see what advantage we can get from it.

1.	P—K4	P—K4
2.	P—Q4	P×P
3.	Q×P	Kt—QB3
4.	Q—K3	Kt—B3

with advantage to Black.

It is scarcely necessary to pursue our analysis any further, for it is evident that Black should have the advantage. He has two Knights in play, while White has achieved nothing but the posting of his Queen in an unfavourable position where she hinders the development of the Queen's Bishop. To sum up, the advance of the Queen's pawn has brought about the exchange of that pawn and the premature development of the Queen ; she soon becomes the target of numerous attacks, each permitting the entry into the game of another enemy piece.

NO. I. POSITION AFTER BLACK'S 4TH MOVE

Nevertheless let us examine whether, in spite of appearances, White cannot obtain an advantage. He has at his disposal two lines of play (a) a direct attack and (b) a normal development.

(a)

| 5. | P—K5 | Kt—KKt5 |
| 6. | Q—K4 | |

QUESTION 1. How should Black continue if, instead, White played 6. Q—K2 ?

6.	....	P—Q4
7.	P×P, *e.p.* ch	B—K3
8.	P×P	Q—Q8 ch
9.	K×Q	Kt×P ch
10.	K—K1	Kt×Q

and Black has a big advantage in development.

We see that as a result of this attack White has no centre at all, for even the King's pawn has disappeared. In the final position White has not developed a single piece and his King has lost the right of castling. On the other hand, Black has developed three pieces, he will soon capture the pawn at his QB2 and has already made the important move P—Q4.

(b)

5.	Kt—QB3	B—Kt5
6.	B—Q2	O—O
7.	O—O—O	R—K1
8.	B—B4	

A Trap! Do not win the pawn by 8. ...., BxKt; 9. BxB, KtxP, for White will obtain a strong attack, *e.g.*, 10. Q—B4, Kt—B3; 11. Kt—B3, P—Q3; 12. Kt—Kt5, B—K3; 13. B—Q3, P—KR3; 14. P—KR4, etc. (Winawer *v.* Steinitz, Nuremburg Tournament, 1896).

8.	....	Kt—K4

QUESTION 2. What continuation do you suggest here for White and for Black ?

This line of play gives Black more difficulty since both sides are equally developed. But this is very much less than in other openings because of the obvious counter-chances. Not only can Black attack White's castled position, but he can speculate on the weakness of the King's pawn. White, to continue his attack, cannot avoid playing P—KB4 and then the King's pawn in an open file will be at the mercy of his opponent. That the pawn can find safety in the advance to K5 is doubtful; on account of the reply P—Q3 it will no longer be secure there. Moreover, the advance to K5 will create strong points for Black at his Q4 and KB4. Nevertheless, we must not think that White's position is desperate; in certain cases he can even stage an attack as is clearly shown by the foregoing trap.

We see then that the premature advance of the Queen's pawn without any preparation, does not achieve its purpose; White does not occupy the centre, Black succeeds in playing P—Q4 and, in general, the result is merely a rapid exchange of the centre pawns.

DANISH GAMBIT

(1. P—K4, P—K4; 2. P—Q4, P×P; 3. P—QB3)

In the previous opening we saw how the premature sortie of his Queen caused White many difficulties. Exposed to the attacks of the enemy, this Queen in the middle of the board only facilitated the development of the hostile pieces. We may ask, therefore, if the fault of the Centre Game does

not lie rather in that premature sortie than in the advance
of the Queen's pawn.   In this case, White would have to
play a sort of gambit by a temporary offer of the Queen's
pawn instead of recapturing it with the Queen, or even a
real gambit involving the sacrifice of one or more pawns.
But can one sacrifice the Queen's pawn with impunity and
break up one's centre in the hope of obtaining compensation
in an attack ?   Black should surely be able to find an
adequate defence, but must not feel obliged to maintain
at all costs the pawn he has gained.   It is much better
to give it back at the opportune moment to equalise the
game than to sustain an attack which may become dangerous.   In general, it is bad policy in the opening to play for
the gain of a pawn and to prefer this inert material to the
advantages of free and active play with the pieces.

1.	P—K4	P—K4
2.	P—Q4	P×P
3.	P—QB3	

QUESTION 3.   What other continuation is possible for
White if he does not wish to sacrifice a second pawn by
3. P—QB3 ?

3.	....	P×P
4.	B—QB4	P×P
5.	B×P	P—Q4
6.	B×QP	Kt—KB3

and the game is about even.

A little trap.   If White plays 7. B×P, ch, Black replies
with 7. .... K×B, since after 8. Q×Q he regains the
Queen by playing 8. .... B—Kt5 ch.

In this opening Black can easily equalise the game by
playing P—Q4 as soon as possible, either at the 3rd or 4th
move, e.g. 3. P—QB3, P—Q4 ; 4. KP×P, Q×P ; 5. P×P,
Kt—QB3 ; 6. Kt—KB3, B—Kt5, etc.   In general, P—Q4
is Black's liberating move as it enables him to destroy
White's centre and to develop his own pieces with ease.
If he prefers a difficult game, but with a pawn ahead, he
need not take the third pawn (4. .... P×P) but simply
play 4. .... P—Q3 and make up his mind to remain on
the defensive.

To avoid the early exchange of pieces, White, at the 6th
move of the main variation, can capture the Queen's pawn

with his King's pawn (6. P×P) instead of with the Bishop, but by so doing, he closes the diagonal from his QR2 to KKt8 which is so important for his attack, and Black gets out of all his difficulties by continuing with 6. .... Kt—KB3 ; 7. Kt—QB3, B—Q3 ; he then has a good game with a pawn ahead.

We see, then, that by a very early P—Q4 White does not prevent Black from freeing his game by P—Q4 and so nullifying the advantage of the move.

PONZIANI'S OPENING

(I. P—K4, P—K4 ; 2. KT—KB3, KT—QB3 ; 3. P—B3)

If, without preparation, the advance P—Q4 gives White no advantage, perhaps the move should be made, after preparation by White to recapture at Q4 with a pawn. Thus we arrive at the move 3. P—B3, which characterises Ponziani's Opening.

As soon as we have made this move, we see its disadvantages ; it is a move with no other threat than the advance of the Queen's pawn (4. P—Q4). Therefore, this preparatory move 3. P—B3 gives Black a tempo of which he should immediately take advantage. Let us see how.

Any amateur of only moderate strength, and even any beginner should already know the move by which Black can take advantage of the unique chance offered to him. For if all the open games centre round White's P—Q4, it is just the same for Black ; already in the previous openings we have seen that Black equalises the game by the advance of his Queen's pawn (P—Q4). This advance is the key to all the open games.

It is rarely that Black is able to do this in advantageous conditions as he is a move behind and his opponent usually does it first. Therefore he must seize his opportunity *at once*. Here the conditions are particularly favourable. By playing P—B3, White has deprived himself of the possibility of bringing out his Queen's Knight to QB3 to attack Black's Queen when she recaptures at Q4 as was the case with White's Queen in the Centre Game. Already, then, we can conclude that the move P—B3 is manifestly bad and that the reply P—Q4 completely refutes Ponziani's Opening.

But the move P—B3, by preventing Kt—QB3, offers

Black yet another possibility ; White's King's pawn, deprived of its natural defence (a Knight at QB3) can be attacked by Kt—B3.

You see then how already, at the 3rd move, Black seizes the initiative. He makes just natural moves, but these moves are extremely strong. This is the consequence of White's too passive play. Moreover 3. P—B3 is a derogation of a fundamental rule in the theory of the openings. We formulate it here with those already mentioned, viz. :

    1.   The rapid development of the pieces.
    2.   The occupation of the centre.
    3.   The general plan.
    4.   The control of the centre.
And now 5.   As far as possible each move in the opening should carry with it one or more threats.

If you do not threaten anything in the opening, you give entire liberty to your opponent not only in the development of his pieces but also in the choice of his threats.

Throughout the game one should harass one's opponent with threats as frequently as possible. In the opening this rule is more than ever true, for there it is absolutely indispensable to prevent him from taking an initiative which frequently proves decisive.

However, one must not imagine that these threats need always be direct or immediate, such as the gain of a pawn, a discovered check, etc. They can be more subtle, or less immediate, or have for their object positional advantage, etc. In the present instance, Black's threat to the King's pawn is obviously more important than White's to advance the Queen's pawn.

Must we conclude, then, that Black has already a won game ? Far from it. In general, except in the case of a gross blunder, a long struggle is necessary to force home a superiority once acquired. Besides, Black, after having surmounted the difficulties presented by a good opening, frequently has to be satisfied with equality and a more or less easy game.

We would add here that these five rules, especially the fifth, are of particular importance in the open games.

Now let us apply these general considerations to some concrete examples :—

(a) STEINITZ'S DEFENCE

1. P—K4   P—K4
2. Kt—KB3   Kt—QB3
3. P—B3   P—Q4

By this quite natural move Black answers the too slow play of his opponent, who already finds himself obliged to alter his plan and seek an advantage by pinning the Queen's Knight.

4. Q—R4

An alternative continuation is 4. B—Kt5, P×P ; 5. Kt×P, Q—Q4 ; 6. Q—R4, Kt—K2 ; 7. P—KB4, B—Q2 ; 8. Kt×B, K×Kt.

4. ....   P—B3
5. B—Kt5   Kt—K2
6. P×P   Q×P
7. P—Q4   B—Q2
8. B—K3   P×P
9. P×P   Kt—K4

A very fine move introduced by Tchigorin. The game is full of possibilities for both sides.

(b) LEONHARDT'S GAMBIT

1. P—K4   P—K4
2. Kt—KB3   Kt—QB3
3. P—B3   P—Q4
4. Q—R4   Kt—B3

Of course, it may seem debatable whether Black is yet justified in embarking on a gambit. However, the attack that he gets must not be under-estimated.

5. Kt×P   B—Q3
6. Kt×Kt

The continuation 6. P×P, B×Kt ; 7. P×Kt, O—O gives Black the better game.

6. ....   P×Kt
7. P—Q4

The continuation 7. P—K5, B×P ; 8. P—Q4, B—Q3 ; 9. Q×P ch, B—Q2 ; 10. Q—R6 has recently been refuted by Alekhine in the following short game :—10. ...., O—O ; 11. B—K2, R—K1 ; 12. Kt—Q2, R—Kt1 ; 13. P—QR4, Q—K2 ; 14. Kt—B1, B—Kt4, and White resigned. (Fink v. Alekhine, Pasadena Tournament, 1932.)

7.	....	P×P
8.	B—QR6	B—Q2
9.	B—Kt7	R—QKt1
10.	B×P	O—O

QUESTION 4.   What defence would you choose for White against Leonhardt's Gambit ?

(c) THE ATTACK ON THE KING'S PAWN

1.	P—K4	P—K4
2.	Kt—KB3	Kt—QB3
3.	P—B3	Kt—B3
4.	P—Q4	Kt×KP
5.	P—Q5	Kt—Kt1

If you are playing against a weak opponent you may well make a pretty combination :—5. ...., B—B4 ; 6. P×Kt, B×P ch ; 7. K—K2, KtP×P ; but if, however, you are White and this gambit is offered to you, refute it by 8. Q—R4, P—KB4 ; 9. QKt—Q2.

6.	B—Q3	Kt—B4
7.	Kt×P	Kt×B, ch
8.	Kt×Kt	P—Q3

The position is even.   Black has no weakness and he has two Bishops.   For these, however, he must find some good squares before White starts an attack against the castled position by either Q—B3 or P—KB4 (followed by P—KKt4).

SCOTCH GAME AND SCOTCH GAMBIT

(1. P—K4, P—K4 ; 2. KT—KB3, KT—QB3 ; 3. P—Q4)

We have seen that P—Q4 was bad for White at the 2nd move and was no better at the 4th.   Could it not be played at the 3rd move ?   Preparation has already been made for it by 2. Kt—KB3, so that if Black exchanges pawns, White retakes with the Knight and not with the Queen, as was the case in the Centre Game.   If, on the other hand, Black does not exchange, but defends his King's pawn by 3. ...., P—Q3, White has then obtained what he sought.   He has two centre pawns on his 4th rank while Black has only one on his 4th and the other on his 3rd.   Here White's advantage is obvious and he can continue with 4. P×P, P×P

(if 4. .... Kt×P, then 5. Kt×Kt, P×Kt; 6. Q×Q ch);
5. Q×Q ch whereupon Black is forced to retake with the
King and lose the right of castling. If, instead, 5. ....
Kt×Q, then 6. Kt×P, winning a pawn.

This variation shows us why Black is forced to exchange
pawns (3. .... P×P) and the result obtained by White
justifies us in considering this opening as superior to those
we have discussed up to now. However, Black once again
can play to attack the somewhat weak King's pawn by
P—Q4 and so equalise the game.

As for White, he has two possible continuations. He can
either recapture the pawn with his Knight (the Scotch
Game) or he can play to further the development of his
pieces by sacrificing the pawn (the Scotch Gambit).

(a) SCOTCH GAME

1.	P—K4	P—K4
2.	Kt—KB3	Kt—QB3
3.	P—Q4	P×P
4.	Kt×P	Kt—B3

An alternative continuation is 4. .... B—B4; 5. B—K3,
B—Kt 3; 6. Kt—QB3, P—Q3, etc.

5. Kt×Kt

5. Kt—QB3 is not so strong. It may lead to the same
variations but it allows Black to avoid them with advantage.
Thus, after 5. Kt—QB3, B—Kt5; 6. Kt×Kt, KtP×Kt;
7. B—Q3, P—Q4; 8. P×P Black can either enter into the
main variation by playing 8. .... P×P or he can force the
exchange of Queens by 8. .... Q—K2 ch.

5.	....	KtP×Kt
6.	B—Q3	P—Q4
7.	P×P	

In passing, let us consider this two-edged continuation :—
7. P—K5, Kt—Kt5; 8. B—KB4, B—QB4; 9. O—O. If
now Black plays 9. .... P—Kt4 (with the intention of
replying to 10. B—Kt3 with an immediate attack by 10.
.... P—KR4), then White plays 10. B—Q2 and it remains
to be seen whether Black's attack on the castled position will
come to a head before the weakness of his King's side can
be exploited by White.

7.	....	P×P
8.	O—O	B—K2
9.	Kt—B3	O—O
10.	B—KKt5	P—B3

with an even game.

In this variation one can sometimes force a draw in an unexpected way. Here are two examples.

NO. 2. POSITION AFTER BLACK'S 12TH MOVE
(Alekhine *v.* Dr. Lasker, Moscow, 1914)

13. B×P, P×B; 14. R×B, P×R; 15. Q—Kt3 ch, K—R1; 16. Q—Kt6 with a draw by perpetual check.

NO. 3. POSITION AFTER BLACK'S 13TH MOVE
(Romanovsky *v.* Capablanca, Moscow Tournament, 1925)

14. B×P, P×B ; 15. Q—K3, B—Q3 ; 16. Q×KRP, R—Kt5 ; 17. Q—Kt5 ch with perpetual check.

(b) SCOTCH GAMBIT

1.	P—K4	P—K4
2.	Kt—KB3	Kt—QB3
3.	P—Q4	P×P
4.	B—QB4	B—B4

4. .... Kt—B3 transposes the game into the Two Knights' Defence (see p. 38).

5.	P—B3	P—Q6

Here also, Kt—B3 can be played. It transposes the game into the Giuoco Piano (see page 29). If, instead, 5. .... P×P, then White obtains a strong attack by 6. Kt×P, P—Q3 ; 7. Q—Kt3, Q—Q2 ; 8. Kt—Q5, KKt—K2 ; 9. Q—B3, O—O ; 10. O—O, etc. To try to maintain the gambit pawn at all costs (by 5. .... P×P) is to go against the essential principle of the theory of the openings.

6.	P—QKt4	B—Kt3
7.	P—QR4	P—QR3
8.	O—O	P—Q3
9.	Q—Kt3	Q—K2
10.	B—KKt5	Kt—B3
11.	QKt—Q2	O—O

with even chances.

VIENNA GAME

(1. P—K4, P—K4 ; 2. KT—QB3)

And now a new idea. If, as we have seen, Black equalises without difficulty once he can play P—Q4, why not prevent that move ? If, at the same time, Black profits by the weakness of White's King's pawn, why not defend it at the beginning of the game ?

These considerations, in fact, form the fundamental idea of the Vienna Game, in which the move 2. Kt—QB3 guards White's King's pawn and prevents Black from playing P—Q4. But hardly have we realised the importance of this than we see its weak point. White, instead of attacking, is on the defensive, and, in spite of the advantage of the move, has abandoned the initiative. Black need only reply, in his

turn, with 2. .... Kt—QB3 to bring about an absolutely
symmetrical position in which White has gained nothing
from his first two moves.   But Black can do even better;
he can seize the initiative that White has abandoned so
imprudently.   He can do this by playing 2. .... Kt—KB3 ;
and this Knight, compared with White's at QB3, will be an
active piece for it attacks the King's pawn which the other
Knight guards and it prepares the advance P—Q4 which
the other prevents.   Admittedly White, in his turn, can
now play Kt—B3 and then, after 3. .... Kt—B3, we have
once again a symmetrical position in which White, although
he has abandoned the initiative, has, nevertheless, the advantage of the move.   Thus we see with what circumspection
Black has to make an attack since White has an extra move
in which to defend himself.

If, after 2. .... Kt—KB3, White does not wish to abandon
the initiative, he must try to turn to account the fact that
Black's King's pawn is undefended.   His being defended,
he can all the more easily attack Black's.   But P—Q4 is
still not good and, as we have just seen, the natural move
3. Kt—B3 gives him nothing.   There remains only P—B4,
a move we have not met hitherto and the consequences of
which will be discussed at length under the King's Gambit
(see p. 57).   For the moment, we will content ourselves
with examining two lines of play for White, one passive and
the other more active.

(a) PASSIVE LINE

1.	P—K4	P—K4
2.	Kt—QB3	Kt—QB3
3.	B—B4	Kt—B3

Do not play 3. .... B—B4, although it appears to be
good if White plays 4. Kt—B3 since Black can play 4. ....
P—Q3, threatening B—KKt5 or Kt—B3.   But White
replies to 3. .... B—B4 with 4. Q—Kt4, forcing a weakening
of the King's side by 4. .... P—KKt3 for, if, instead, 4. ....
Q—B3, then White wins quite easily :   5. Kt—Q5, Q×P ch ;
6. K—Q1, K—B1 ;   7. Kt—R3, Q—Q5 ;   8. P—Q3 with a
decisive attack.

4.	P—Q3	B—Kt5
5.	B—KKt5	

If 5. Kt—K2, then Black at once plays 5. .... P—Q4 (a good example of the possibilities which we have discussed at length in the introduction to this opening).

5.	P—KR3
6. B×Kt	B×Kt ch

Beware ! Do not play Q×B before making this move because after 6. .... Q×B ; 7. Kt—K2, P—Q3 ; 8. O—O, etc. Black has a difficult game, the two threats P—B4 and Kt—Q5 being hard to meet.

7. P×B	Q×B
8. Kt—K2	P—Q3

The position is almost even. It seems that after 9. O—O Black is forced to play 9. .... P—KKt4 to prevent 10. P—B4.

QUESTION 5. How would you then continue for White ?

(b) ACTIVE LINE

1. P—K4	P—K4
2. Kt—QB3	Kt—KB3

After this move White cannot prevent the threatened P—Q4 by playing 3. B—B4 because after 3. .... Kt×P ; 4. Kt×Kt Black can—and does—make that move. This variation shows clearly the force of an active move (Kt—KB3) made at the right time.

3. P—B4	P—Q4
4. BP×P	Kt×P
5. Kt—B3	

5. Q—B3 and 5. P—Q3 give rise to two well-known traps.

(1) After 5. Q—B3, Kt—QB3 White must not play to win a pawn by 6. Kt×Kt because of 6. .... Kt—Q5 ; 7. Q—Q3, P×Kt ; 8. Q×P, B—KB4 followed by Kt×P ch. He should, instead, play 6. B—Kt5, Kt×Kt ; 7. KtP×Kt, Q—R 5 ch ; 8. P—Kt3, Q—K 5 ch ; 9. Q×Q, P×Q with an even game.

(2) After 5. P—Q3 Black must not play 5. .... Q—R 5 ch ; 6. P—Kt3, Kt×P because of 7. Kt—B3, Q—R4 ; 8. Kt×P, Kt×R ; 9. Kt×P ch, K—Q1 ; 10. Kt×R. He should, instead, play 5. .... Kt×Kt ; 6. P×Kt, B—K2 ; 7. Kt—B3, O—O ; 8. P—Q4, P—KB3 and will have a good game.

5.	....	B—K2
6.	P—Q4	O—O
7.	B—Q3	P—B4
8.	P×P, *e.p.*	Kt×Kt
9.	P×Kt	B×P
10.	O—O	Kt—B3

with an even game.

For those who want an early draw the following continuation may be mentioned : 1. P—K4, P—K4 ; 2. Kt—QB3, Kt—KB3 ; 3. P—B4, P—Q4 ; 4. BP×P, Kt×P ; 5. P—Q3, Kt×Kt ; 6. P×Kt, B—K2 ; 7. P—Q4, O—O ; 8. B—Q3, P—KB3 ; 9. Q—R5, P—KKt3 ; 10. B×P, P×B ; 11. Q×Pch, K—R1 ; 12. Q—R 6 ch, with perpetual check.

PETROFF'S DEFENCE

(1. P—K4, P—K4 ; 2. KT—KB3, KT—KB3)

A bold player, as Black, having come to the conclusion that many openings give White no advantage, might well ask himself why Black should not, instead of defending, venture at once upon an aggressive game. Is the move such an advantage ? Have we not, for example, the case of the Opposition where the advantage is with the player without the move ? Is not the initial symmetrical position, also, a problem in opposition, whose solution should be found in not disturbing the equilibrium ?

Certainly one can have nothing but admiration for such a bold idea, especially in these days when timidity is too often the characteristic of chess players : but this would be to misjudge the very principles of the game rather than to discover a semblance of truth in what is, in the main, a paradox. The number of men and the variety of moves in the initial position make it difficult to consider it as a case of Opposition. Further, White can easily make quiet waiting moves which allow the advantage of the move to pass to his opponent or else lead once again to symmetry.

Moreover, experience shows us that, in practice, it is impossible to maintain the symmetry of the position by copying one's opponent's moves, for, at a given moment, the move leads by force to an advantage.

It cannot then be a question of Opposition in the symmetrical positions of the opening.

In Petroff's Defence, Black seizes the initiative on the second move. But White, with a move ahead, has no difficulty whatever in maintaining equilibrium, and Black, if he persists in his intention of attacking, will be forced to play some kind of gambit with all its attendant risks.

(a) THE REGULAR DEFENCE

1.	P—K4	P—K4
2.	Kt—KB3	Kt—KB3
3.	Kt×P	

QUESTION 6. How would you continue after the gambit move 3. B—B4 ?

3.	....	P—Q3

Beware of a terrible blunder here ! Black cannot immediately recapture the pawn by 3. .... Kt×P without losing the game. White plays 4. Q—K2 ! and the Knight cannot move because of 5. Kt—B 6 ch ; therefore either it must be defended by 4. .... P—Q4 (to which White replies with 5. P—Q3) or Black must make a counter-attack on White's Knight by 4. .... Q—K2. The continuation is 5. Q×Kt, P—Q3 ; 6. P—Q4, P—KB3 ; 7. P—KB4 and White gains at least a pawn.

4.	Kt—KB3	Kt×P
5.	P—Q4	P—Q4
6.	B—Q3	Kt—QB3
7.	O—O	B—K2
8.	R—K1	B—KKt5
9.	P—B3	P—B4

You see that in this opening Black all the time endeavours to forestall White with threats and avoids merely developing moves (e.g., O—O) which would allow White to recapture the initiative.

(b) MARSHALL'S GAMBIT

1.	P—K4	P—K4
2.	Kt—KB3	Kt—KB3
3.	Kt×P	

Here is a simpler continuation leading to a symmetrical position : 3. P—Q4, Kt×P ; 4. B—Q3, P—Q4 ; 5. Kt×P, B—Q3 ; 6. O—O, O—O, etc.

3.	....	P—Q3
4.	Kt—KB3	Kt×P
5.	P—Q4	P—Q4
6.	B—Q3	B—Q3
7.	O—O	B—KKt5
8.	P—B4	O—O
9.	P×P	P—KB4
10.	Kt—B3	Kt—Q2

PHILIDOR'S DEFENCE

(1. P—K4, P—K4 ; 2. KT—KB3, P—Q3)

In contrast to the aggressive Petroff's Defence, Philidor's Defence appears almost too passive. To resign oneself to the move P—Q3 without being forced, to give up without reason the chance of playing the pawn to Q4 in one move, and, even if Black cannot always succeed in forcing P—Q4, not even to wait till the opening has taken shape before deciding on the timid defence P—Q3—all these points speak against Philidor's Defence, which, moreover, has for its only object the defence of the King's pawn and in so doing permanently limits the action of the King's Bishop.

In spite of all these good reasons, P—Q3 is not a bad move ; it in no way weakens the position and allows Black to avoid several difficult openings. Philidor's Defence is based on a passive and slow game. We may add, that in allowing White to play P—Q4 at the 3rd move, Black practically commits himself to an immediate exchange of pawns which appears contrary to the idea of holding on to the centre, the idea which 2. .... P—Q3 obviously implies. If Black wishes to hold on to the centre at all costs, he must build up quite a new defence and make unusual moves without, however, being sure of obtaining equality.

Let us look, then, at the two ways of treating this defence : (a) The exchange of pawns ; (b) The defence of the King's pawn at all costs (Hanham Variation).

(a) THE EXCHANGE OF PAWNS

| 1. | P—K4 | P—K4 |
| 2. | Kt—KB3 | P—Q3 |

Beware ! Here is a blunder to be avoided and also an example of an insufficient defence with a pawn. Black

cannot defend the King's pawn by 2. .... P—KB3 without
soon losing the game, *e.g.*, 3. Kt×P !, P×Kt; 4. Q—R 5 ch,
P—Kt3 (if 4. .... K—K2 ; then 5. Q×P ch, K—B2 ;
6. B—B4 ch, P—Q4 ; 7. B×P ch, K—Kt3 ; 8. B×P, and
wins); 5. Q×KP ch, followed by 6. Q×R. To avoid this
débâcle Black should play 3. .... Q—K2. The continuation
is 4. Kt—KB3, Q×P ch ; 5. B—K2, and White has much
the better game. Even if it did not permit this combination,
the move 2. .... P—KB3 would be bad, because it weakens
the castled position and increases the value of White's King's
Bishop when it is posted at QB4.

3.	P—Q4	P×P
4.	Kt×P	Kt—KB3
5.	Kt—QB3	B—K2

We have now variations more or less similar to those of
the Scotch Game, with this difference, all to the disadvantage
of Black, that his King's Bishop cannot play to QKt5. He
will therefore be forced to lose a valuable tempo in playing
P—Q4. On the other hand, White is not compelled to play
B—QKt5 but can place his Bishop on a better square according to necessity. Already we know that a large choice of
moves is an advantage ; when the choice becomes more
restricted, the position is already inferior.

(b) HANHAM VARIATION

1.	P—K4	P—K4
2.	Kt—KB3	P—Q3
3.	P—Q4	Kt—Q2
4.	B—QB4	P—QB3

Why does Black play P—QB3 in this opening ? Because
he is threatened with 5. P×P, P×P ; 6. Q—Q5. We see
also that Kt—Q2 shuts in the Queen's Bishop just as P—Q3
does the King's Bishop. Furthermore, wishing to maintain
the King's pawn at all costs, Black proposes to protect it
again by Q—B2. But all these preparations cost too much
time and compromise Black's game.

5.	O—O

Another very good continuation is 5. Kt—Kt5, Kt—R3 ;
6. O—O, B—K2 ; 7. Kt—K6, P×Kt ; 8. B×Kt, Kt—Kt3 ;
9. B×KtP, etc., a combination which frequently occurs in
this variation of Philidor's Defence. It is preferable for

White to play Kt—Kt5 before Black's Bishop goes to K2, because if the Bishop is already there as in the main variation, Black can play (instead of 7. .... Kt—R3) 7. .... B×Kt with the continuation 8. Q—R5, P—KKt3 ; 9. Q×B, which gives White the better ending but the win is still far off.

Beware ! A very subtle trap. If after 5. Kt—Kt5, Kt—R3 ; White plays 6. P—QR4 ! Black in making the natural move 6. .... B—K2 will fall into a trap.

NO. 4. POSITION AFTER BLACK'S 6TH MOVE

7. B×P ch, Kt×B ; 8. Kt—K6, Q—Kt3 ; 9. P—R5, Q—Kt 5 ch ; 10. B—Q2, Q—B5 ; 11. Kt—B7 ch, K—Q1 ; 12. P—QKt3, winning the Queen. The squares KB2 and K3 are very weak for Black in this opening. Moreover, his moves P—Q3 and Kt—Q2, devoid of any threat, leave White plenty of time to construct a winning position.

5.	....	B—K2
6.	P×P	P×P
7.	Kt—Kt5	Kt—R3
8.	Kt—K6	P×Kt
9.	B×Kt	Kt—Kt3
10.	Q—R5 ch	K—B1
11.	P—B4	

with a winning attack.

Let us now look at the consequences of an error of judgment. If after having chosen a slow defence like Philidor's,

Black attempts to free himself too quickly and to adopt a more active policy, he runs the risk of losing the game, *e.g.*, 1. P—K4, P—K4 ; 2. Kt—KB3, P—Q3 ; 3. P—Q4, B—Kt5 ; 4. P×P, B×Kt ; 5. Q×B, P×P ; 6. B—QB4, Kt—KB3 ; 7. Q—QKt3, Q—K2.

NO 5.   POSITION AFTER BLACK'S 7TH MOVE

In this position Morphy, in a celebrated game, forced a win as follows : 8. Kt—B3, P—B3 ; 9. B—KKt5, P—Kt4 ; 10. Kt×P, P×Kt ; 11. B×KtP ch, QKt—Q2 ; 12. O—O—O, R—Q1 ; 13. R×Kt, R×R ; 14. R—Q1, Q—K3 ; 15. B×R ch, Kt×B ; 16. Q—Kt8 ch, Kt×Q ; 17. R—Q8 mate.

GIUOCO PIANO

(1. P—K4, P—K4 ; 2. KT—KB3, KT—QB3 ; 3. B—B4, B—B4)

We come at last to an opening which follows, at any rate partially, the rules which we have enunciated earlier in the book. We can therefore already assert its superiority over the openings examined up to now. However, the third move, B—B4, threatens nothing and White thus allows Black the choice of several moves. The first of these that comes to mind is Kt—KB3, attacking the King's pawn ; it will be analysed in the next section since it constitutes a separate opening, the Two Knights' Defence. For the moment we will look at the less enterprising move B—B4.

First of all, what is the object of the move 3. B—B4 ? It prevents P—Q4, but that is a purely negative idea ; moreover, Black is not yet threatening that move. 3. B—B4 does not seem a preparation for P—Q4, and even if it threatens the King's Bishop's pawn, it must be admitted that this attack only succeeds in very special cases, since that pawn is very well defended after Black has castled.

The object of the move 3. B—B4 is not obvious and its value consists entirely in its complexity. By this purely developing move White confronts Black with the serious problem of what reply to choose. After 3. .... Kt—B3, the attack on the King's Bishop's pawn by 4. Kt—Kt5 may become effective. After 3. .... P—Q3, Black's King's Bishop is shut in, and we have once again the inconveniences of Philidor's Defence. Finally, if Black decides in favour of 4. .... B—B4, the threat of P—Q4 gains in strength, for there the pawn will attack not only the King's pawn but the Bishop.

This is the essential difference between White's position and Black's : the latter not having yet played Kt—B3 does not threaten to play P—Q4 for a long time, whereas White, on the contrary, can play P—Q4 without any difficulty.

In spite of the symmetry, the positions of the two Bishops are in no way equivalent ; Black's can quickly be attacked by P—Q4, White's has not that move to fear. *Duo si faciunt idem, non est idem.* To sum up 3. B—B4 indirectly prepares the advance P—Q4. But Black is not without defence. We have seen that 3. .... B—B4 is the natural reply and it should, therefore, not be abandoned, more especially as it enforces further preparation for the move P—Q4, thus compelling White to make a second move without a direct threat. It seems very unlikely that Black will not be able to find a satisfactory defence.

Black can defend passively, in which case he will do everything possible to maintain his King's pawn. If he prefers a more active and open game, he should exchange that pawn, for this will allow him to make a counter-attack on White's King's pawn by Kt—B3 and to prepare to play P—Q4. At the moment he seeks only equality and should not yet dream of superiority. If White welcomes all these complications he will play P—Q4 after further preparation ; if he wishes to avoid them he will play a closer game and content himself with P—Q3.

There are thus three methods of procedure in this opening (a) Passive play by White, (b) Passive play by Black, (c) Active play.

Some of the variations in the third category, *e.g.*, the Möller Attack, have the gambit character, and we shall meet a real gambit, the Evans, of quite a new type.

(a) PASSIVE PLAY BY WHITE
(GIUOCO PIANISSIMO)

1.	P—K4	P—K4
2.	Kt—KB3	Kt—QB3
3.	B—B4	B—B4
4.	P—Q3	Kt—B3
5.	Kt—B3	P—Q3

Observe the completely symmetrical position after Black's 5th move. This way of treating the opening by White cannot be the best because it does nothing to increase the advantage of the move and so Black's play presents no difficulty. We need only make a few remarks to guide both players. If, in this or in analogous positions, your opponent plays B—K3, you should not exchange Bishops. It is much better to retire your Bishop to Kt3 or even to leave it at B4. If you exchange Bishops, you double your opponent's pawns but at the same time you open for him the King's Bishop's file and this will become a valuable aid in the attack on your castled position. Moreover, the pawn at K3 provides a good defence for the square Q4 so that the centre is well guarded and under observation. If you begin an attack by P—KB4 or P—Q4, you undouble his pawns and allow him to play P—K4 and at the same time the King's Bishop's file remains open.

Beware ! In positions of this kind do not be in a hurry to castle, or else the pin on your King's Knight by B—KKt5 may be very embarrassing. Thus the preventive move P—KR3 is indicated. After having castled, do not pin your opponent's King's Knight if he has not castled, for then he will seize the initiative.

NO. 6.　POSITION AFTER 5. O—O, P—Q3

6.	B—KKt5	P—KR3
7.	B—R4	P—KKt4

He who has not castled can make this advance (P—KR3 and P—KKt4) since he has the possibility of castling on the Queen's side ; but he who has castled cannot thus free himself from the pin for he will weaken too much his castled position.

| 8. | B—KKt3 | P—KR4 |

A bold idea, due to Steinitz.　It has not been refuted.

9.	Kt×KtP	P—R5
10.	Kt×P	P×B
11.	Kt×Q	B—KKt5
12.	Q—Q2	Kt—Q5
13.	Kt—B3	

QUESTION 7.　Can you find a better defence for White here ?

13.	....	Kt—B6 ch
14.	P×Kt	B×P

and Black wins.

(b) GIUOCO PIANO

1.	P—K4	P—K4
2.	Kt—KB3	Kt—QB3
3.	B—B4	B—B4
4.	P—B3	Kt—B3

If Black prefers a passive game, he should avoid at all

costs the exchange of his King's pawn and should guard it by 4. .... Q—K2. However, after 5. P—Q4, B—Kt3 ; 6. O—O, Kt—B3 ; 7. R—K1, P—Q3 ; 8. P—KR3, O—O he has a difficult game.

5.	P—Q4	P×P
6.	P×P	B—Kt5 ch
7.	B—Q2	

7. Kt—B3 leads to the Möller Attack, which we shall analyse later.

7.	....	B×B ch
8.	QKt×B	P—Q4

We see that Black has succeeded in making this move—and even without having had to prepare it (as White did by P—B3). Therefore, Black has gained time and secured equality.

9.	P×P	KKt×P
10.	Q—Kt3	

It is essential to make this move before castling, otherwise Black, after also castling and so guarding his King's Bishop's pawn, will not be forced to guard the Knight at his Q4 after White plays Q—Kt3 but will simply move it away.

10.	....	QKt—K2
11.	O—O	O—O
12.	KR—K1	P—QB3

Black has completed his development and, in spite of the weaknesses at his K4 and QB4, has an even game since White's Queen's pawn is isolated.

QUESTION 8. How would you continue this variation for White ?

(c) MÖLLER ATTACK

1.	P—K4	P—K4
2.	Kt—KB3	Kt—QB3
3.	B—B4	B—B4
4.	P—B3	Kt—B3
5.	P—Q4	P×P
6.	P×P	B—Kt5 ch
7.	Kt—B3	Kt×KP
8.	O—O	B×Kt

The simplest way to avoid the Möller Attack is to play Bernstein's variation : 8. .... Kt×Kt ; 9. P × Kt, B×P ;

10. Q—Kt3, P—Q4 (for the consequences of 10. .... B×R, see p. 35); 11. B×P, O—O and Black has an even game. If 12. B×P ch, then 12. .... K—R1.

9. P—Q5

This is Möller's Attack. Formerly Steinitz's Attack was played, *viz.*, 9. P×B, P—Q4 ; 10. B—R3. Black having played P—Q4, White's attack has no chance of coming to anything.

9.	....	B—B3
10.	R—K1	Kt—K2
11.	R×Kt	P—Q3

If Black castles at once, White can, if he wishes, force a draw at once : 11. .... O—O ; 12. P—Q6, P×P ; 13. Q×P, Kt—B4 ; 14. Q—Q5, Kt—K2 ; 15. Q—Q6, etc.

12.	B—Kt5	B×B
13.	Kt×B	O—O
14.	Kt×RP	K×Kt
15.	Q—R5 ch	K—Kt1
16.	R—R4	P—KB4
17.	R—K1	

Stronger than 17. Q—R7 ch, K—B2 ; 18. R—R6, R—KKt1 ; 19. R—K1, K—B1, etc.

17.	....	Kt—Kt3
18.	R—R3	R—B3

QUESTION 9. How would you continue this variation for White ?

We now give Greco's famous trap.

NO. 7. POSITION AFTER WHITE'S 10TH MOVE

If, in Bernstein's variation (see note to Black's 8th move in the Möller Attack, p. 33) Black, instead of playing 10. .... P—Q4, captures the Rook, he loses at once :—

10. .... B×R ? ; 11. B×P ch, K—B1 ; 12. B—Kt5, Kt—K2 ; 13. Kt—K5, B×P ; 14. B—Kt6, P—Q4 ; 15. Q—B3 ch, B—B4 ; 16. B×B, B×Kt ; 17. B—K6 ch, B—B3 ; 18. B×B, and wins.

EVANS GAMBIT

(1. P—K4, P—K4 ; 2. KT—KB3, KT—QB3 ; 3. B—B4, B—B4 ; 4. P—QKT4)

Already in some gambits we have seen the sacrifice of one or more pawns for the purpose of obtaining an advantage over the opponent in development. But the gain of a single tempo in return for the pawn sacrificed is not sufficient to justify the gambit, for a pawn is worth more than a tempo. One must either gain several tempi or else obtain compensation for the lost pawn in positional advantage, *i.e.*, gain also in space. In the Danish Gambit White sacrifices all his important centre pawns but does not gain much time, for each capture by Black has followed an advance of the pawn sacrificed. It is this fact that renders that gambit incorrect. In general, the capture of a sacrificed pawn by a pawn does not provide the gambit player with as much advantage in time as does the capture with a piece, for the latter may be exposed to various attacks which will occasion further loss of time.

The Evans Gambit is brought about by the sacrifice of a wing pawn and therein is an advantage over the other gambits because a wing pawn has less material importance than a centre one. Moreover, the pawn sacrificed is captured by a Bishop which we can then attack with pawn moves which are very useful for our advance in the centre. Already we see that in this gambit White, although sacrificing very little material, gains several tempi and secures for himself the complete occupation of the centre. Black, on the other hand, is generally unable to play the freeing move P—Q4 and has to defend with great care. However, he will follow the principles we have already enunciated and will attempt to complete his development as soon as possible without trying to maintain the pawn gained at all costs. On the contrary, he must not hesitate to give back the pawn if by so doing he can break the attack, the more especially as the absence of one pawn from the Queen's side and the isolation of another will render White's position in the end-game very precarious.

(a) EVANS GAMBIT ACCEPTED

1.	P—K4	P—K4
2.	Kt—KB3	Kt—QB3
3.	B—B4	B—B4
4.	P—QKt4	

This, although not a change of plan, is a distinct deviation from normal opening play. White delays playing P—Q4 for one or two moves to assure himself the occupation of the centre without loss of time.

> 4. ....   B×P

If Black does not take the pawn, he still has many difficulties to overcome. This line of play, the Evans Gambit Declined, we shall analyse later.

> 5. P—B3   B—R4

This retreat is preferable to B—B4 after which move White, by playing P—Q4, would force the Bishop to make a further retreat.

> 6. P—Q4

Better than 6. O—O, in reply to which Black can play Lasker's Defence, 6. .... P—Q3 ; 7. P—Q4, B—Kt3.

> 6. ....   P×P

6. .... P—Q3 ; 7. O—O, B—Kt3 would transpose into Lasker's Defence, but White can avoid this by playing 7. Q—Kt3, Q—Q2 ; 8. P—QR4, etc.

> 7. O—O   B—Kt3

The continuation 7. .... P×P ; 8. Q—Kt3, Q—B3 ; 9. P—K5, Q—Kt3 ; 10. Kt×P, KKt—K2 ; 11. B—R3 gives White a strong attack.

> 8. P×P   P—Q3

We have now the "Normal Position."

NO. 8.   POSITION AFTER BLACK'S 8TH MOVE

White has the choice of three continuations : 9. B—Kt2,
9. Kt—B3 and 9. P—Q5. He occupies the centre and has
an advantage of a tempo, but Black's position has no sign
of weakness and can be defended.

QUESTION 10.   How would you continue against Lasker's
Defence (see p. 36) ?

(b) EVANS GAMBIT DECLINED

1.	P—K4	P—K4
2.	Kt—KB3	Kt—QB3
3.	B—B4	B—B4
4.	P—QKt4	B—Kt3
5.	P—Kt5	Kt—R4
6.	Kt×P	Kt—R3

The best move. 6. .... Q—B3 and 6. .... Q—Kt4
are inferior because of 7. B×P ch, K—B1 ; 8. B×Kt,
Q×Kt ; 9. B—Q5, P—B3 ; 10. Q—B3 ch, etc.

Beware ! You must not think that the following combination to gain White's Queen's Rook is correct : 6. .... Kt×B ;
7. Kt×Kt, B×P ch ; 8. K×B, Q—B3 ch ; 9. Q—B3, and
Black cannot take the Rook since after 9. .... Q×R ;
10. Kt—B3 the Queen cannot escape.

7.	P—Q4	P—Q3
8.	B×Kt	P×Kt
9.	B×P	R—KKt1
10.	B×P ch	K×B
11.	B×P	Q—Kt4

In spite of his four pawns for the piece, White's game is compromised since the position of his King is very exposed.

TWO KNIGHTS' DEFENCE

(1. P—K4, P—K4 ; 2. KT—KB3, KT—QB3 ; 3. B—B4, KT—B3)

In any opening in which Black tries at all costs to seize the initiative he is involved in a game which is full of dangers —the natural consequence of his being a move behind. This we shall find is the characteristic of the Two Knights' Defence in which Black, instead of making the quiet and plausible move 3. .... B—B4 (bringing about the Giuoco Piano) adventures on an active game by attacking White's King's pawn by 3. .... Kt—B3. Admittedly White has made in 3. B—B4 a move without any threat, but, nevertheless, it is a good developing move. Without blaming Black for his boldness in seizing an opportunity to take the initiative, we cannot avoid taxing him with imprudence for already we know that Kt—KB3 allows White immediately to attack the King's Bishop's pawn by Kt—Kt5. Moreover, White can, instead, take possession of the centre by P—Q4. As for the counter-attack on White's K4, it is very dangerous for Black since he is not yet ready to castle and thus the opening of the file would be all to the advantage of White. It follows that the Two Knights' Defence may give rise to all sorts of sacrifices, by one player or the other. If White contents himself with a quiet game, he will not obtain the advantage which he may anticipate from Black's imprudence. Black, on the other hand, has no choice ; after his 3rd move he cannot draw back but must engage in a dangerous combinative game.

There are two ways in which White may treat this opening :

(1) 4. P—Q4 with an attack in the centre and eventually some sacrifices.

(2) 4. Kt—Kt5 with an attack on the King's Bishop's pawn. In this line of play it is Black who has the initiative but at the cost of a pawn.

4. P—Q4 leads to the celebrated Max Lange Attack. Black can either defend patiently against this attack or can avoid it.

(a) MAX LANGE ATTACK

1.	P—K4	P—K4
2.	Kt—KB3	Kt—QB3
3.	B—B4	Kt—B3
4.	P—Q4	P×P
5.	O—O	B—B4

It is here that Black can avoid the Max Lange Attack—by taking the second pawn. We give this variation later.

6.	P—K5	P—Q4
7.	P×Kt	P×B
8.	R—K1 ch	B—K3

After 8. .... K—B1, White wins by 9. B—Kt5, P—KKt3 ; 10. B—R6 ch, K—Kt1 ; 11. Kt—B3.

9.	Kt—Kt5	Q—Q4

Beware of the following trap ! If 9. .... Q×P ?, then 10. Kt×B, P×Kt ; 11. Q—R5 ch, followed by 12. Q×B, winning a piece.

10.	Kt—QB3	Q—B4
11.	QKt—K4	O—O—O

Other defences are no better, e.g. :—

(1) 11. .... B—Kt3 ; 12. P×P, R—KKt1 ; 13. P—KKt4, Q—Kt3 ; 14. Kt×B, P×Kt ; 15. B—Kt5.

(2) 11. .... B—KB1 ; 12. Kt×BP, K×Kt ; 13. Kt—Kt5 ch, K—Kt1 ; 14. P—KKt4, Q—Q4 ; 15. R×B

12.	Kt×QB	P×Kt
13.	P—KKt4	Q—K4
14.	P×P	

White has deferred the capture of this pawn as long as possible. Made earlier, it would have rendered Black's defence easier.

14.	....	KR—Kt1
15.	B—R6	

This move, which defends the pawn at Kt7 and immobilises the hostile King's Rook, increases Black's difficulties, in spite of his semblance of attack.

15.	....	P—Q6
16.	P—B3	

and Black will have all the difficulty in the world to save the game. He is threatened with P—Kt5 and also with Q—B3 followed by Kt—B6 with the immediate gain of the exchange.

QUESTION 11. What continuation to this line of play do you suggest ?

(b) THE MAX LANGE ATTACK AVOIDED

1.	P—K4	P—K4
2.	Kt—KB3	Kt—QB3
3.	B—B4	Kt—B3
4.	P—Q4	P×P
5.	O—O	Kt×P
6.	R—K1	P—Q4
7.	B×P	

Canal's Attack (7. Kt—B3 followed, if 7. .... P×Kt, by 8. B×P) does not seem to increase White's attacking chances and complicates the game unnecessarily. Black does best to transpose into the main line by 7. .... P×B ; 8. R×Kt ch, B—K2 ; 9. Kt×P, P—B4 ; 10. R—B4, O—O, etc.

7.	....	Q×B
8.	Kt—B3	Q—Q1

8. .... Q—QR4 also gives a more or less even game, e.g., 8. .... Q—QR4 ; 9. Kt×Kt (or 9. R×Kt ch, B—K3 ; 10. Kt×P, O—O—O), B—K3 and White can now develop his Queen's Bishop at Q2 without any loss of time.

9.	R×Kt ch	B—K2

Black makes rapid preparations to castle on the King's side, castling on the other side having become impossible.

10.	Kt×P	P—B4
11.	R—B4	O—O

Black has surmounted the difficulties of the opening. His pawns are weak, but in return he has two Bishops.

QUESTION 12. What would you do with the Rook at B4 in this variation ?

(c) TWO KNIGHTS' DEFENCE PROPER

1.	P—K4	P—K4
2.	Kt—KB3	Kt—QB3
3.	B—B4	Kt—B3
4.	Kt—Kt5	P—Q4
5.	P×P	Kt—QR4

Beware ! A trap into which most players have fallen several times in their lives. Black cannot immediately capture the Queen's pawn without losing the game, e.g., 5. .... Kt×P ;

6. Kt×BP (or more quietly, 6. P—Q4 !), K×Kt;
7. Q—B3 ch, K—K3 ; 8. Kt—B3, Kt—K2 ; 9. P—Q4,
P—B3 ; 10. B—KKt 5, etc.

QUESTION 13. If Black played 8. .... Kt—Kt5 (instead
of 8. .... Kt—K2), how would you continue for White ?

6.	B—Kt5 ch	P—B3
7.	P×P	P×P
8.	B—K2	P—KR3
9.	Kt—KB3	P—K5
10.	Kt—K5	B—Q3
11.	P—Q4	Q—B2
12.	B—Q2	

White gives back the pawn he has gained but maintains
the better game.

QUESTION 14. How would you continue the attack for
Black if White played 12. P—KB4 ?

RUY LOPEZ

(1. P—K4, P—K4 ; 2. KT—KB3, KT—QB3 ; 3. B—KT5)

Of all the openings that we have met up to now not one
has completely satisfied White's requirements. In every
case Black has secured a more or less even game and, if in
certain cases equality has seemed more difficult to obtain,
this has been due either to imprudence on the part of Black
or because the game has taken such a complicated turn that
to form a definite conclusion has been difficult.

Thus it is not without fear that we approach the Ruy
Lopez since, if this opening does not satisfy us, we shall have
to seek a solution in the close games or even in bizarre gambits.

The Ruy Lopez has the advantage of maintaining the
tension in the centre for a long time, while in many variations
preventing Black from making the advance P—Q4. Moreover, the threat underlying this opening, far from being
evident, is so hidden as to keep Black busy for a long time.

Of course, the idea of the move 3. B—Kt5 is not the
immediate gain of the King's pawn, for even supposing that
Black did not make a move, after 4. B×Kt, QP×B ; 5. Kt×P,
Q—Q5 White's King's pawn is lost. Nevertheless, this
fictitious threat cannot be completely ignored. Suppose,
for example, that after 3. .... Kt—B3 ; 4. P—Q3 Black

continued his development by 4. .... B—K2. Then, since White's King's pawn is defended, he can gain Black's. Moreover, 3. .... P—Q4 is not possible ; White's Knight on capturing the King's pawn would attack Black's pinned Knight a second time so that Black would be forced to defend it before thinking of winning back the pawn he had lost.

Naturally the value of an opening cannot be based upon the result of a great mistake, but Black's inability to play P—Q4 is of great importance and forces him to fall back on P—Q3, a move whose inconveniences we have already seen in Philidor's Defence. To sum up : the first advantage to White is that he can quickly play P—Q4, whereas Black cannot and is forced to content himself with the modest P—Q3. A second advantage to White—and the logical consequence of the first—is that Black's P—Q3 shuts in his King's Bishop which has no move other than the passive B—K2. White's, on the other hand, is already developed at QKt5. To Black's badly-developed King's Bishop White opposes a very active one. White maintains the advantage of the move, gains in space, and his King's Bishop is stronger than Black's. Can one expect more from an opening after only a few moves ? This is why the Ruy Lopez has always been considered—and justly so—as one of the best openings.

Can we then already conclude that White has a won game ? If this were so, then nothing but the Ruy Lopez would be played in tournaments. Luckily the game depends upon more weighty matters than a sortie of a Bishop to QKt5. Moreover, no weakness can be found in Black's position. White must then progress very slowly under pain of losing all his advantage. As for Black, he must be patient, hold back his counter-attack and defend till the time that White's advantage has gradually disappeared or until in his precipitation he has created some weaknesses in his position.

Black has two ways of treating this very difficult opening. Confident in the strength of his position, he can decide upon a purely passive defence and maintain the centre. Alternatively he can play for a counter-attack on the little weaknesses in White's position. In this case he has the choice either of an attack on White's King's pawn, which is defenceless in a file that can always be opened, or of an advance on the Queen's side, thus taking advantage of the exposed position of White's King's Bishop. Finally, he can combine these two systems.

We shall, therefore, divide the defences most frequently played into two groups :—

(a) ACTIVE DEFENCES

(1) Black plays his King's Bishop to QB4—the Classical Defence—with a variation of it—the Möller Defence ;

(2) Black attacks the King's pawn—the Berlin Defence ;

(3) Black develops his Queen's pawn at Q4—the Morphy Defence.

(b) PASSIVE DEFENCES

(1) Absolutely passive—the Steinitz Defence ;

(2) A passive defence with a counter-attack on the Queen's side—a variation of the Morphy Defence.

We shall not analyse the numerous other defences, since it is much better to understand and remember well the principal ones than to plunge into a sea of variations. We shall make only one exception, and shall consider the Siesta Gambit which is now very common and gives an extremely interesting game.

We will begin with the active defences since thus we shall be able to understand why the passive ones are generally preferred.

(a) ACTIVE DEFENCES
(1) MÖLLER DEFENCE

This defence obviates one of the greatest disadvantages that Black labours under in the Ruy Lopez, *viz.*, the imprisonment of his King's Bishop by the move P—Q3. Black develops his King's Bishop at QB4 at the fifth move (to do it before is not so good), the order of the moves being 1. P—K4, P—K4 ; 2. Kt—KB3, Kt—QB3 ; 3. B—Kt5, P—QR3 ; 4. B—R4, Kt—B3 ; 5. O—O, B—B4. Let us first of all be clear as to the importance of this order of moves. (1) Black's King's Bishop, when attacked by P—Q4, can retreat to QR2 where it will not hinder the advance of the Queen's Knight's pawn and will not be exposed to the possibility of being exchanged for the hostile Queen's Knight by Kt—QR4 as it would be at QKt3. (2) Black, having an attack on the King's pawn, is no longer forced to abandon the centre by replying to P—Q4 by P×P ; and finally (3)

Black is ready to castle and so the opening of the King's file no longer threatens danger to him.

However, even in this form, the sortie of the King's Bishop has its drawbacks, for the castled position is deprived of an important defensive piece, and the action of the Bishop on White's King's Bishop's pawn cannot be effective till much later in the game.

Now let us look at the principal variation of this defence :

1.	P—K4	P—K4
2.	Kt—KB3	Kt—QB3
3.	B—Kt5	P—QR3

QUESTION 15. How should White reply if Black played 3. .... B—B4 (the Classical Defence) ?

4.	B—R4	Kt—B3
5.	O—O	B—B4
6.	P—B3	B—R2
7.	P—Q4	Kt×KP
8.	P×P	

Better than 8. Q—K2, P—B4 ; 9. P×P, O—O. However, 8. R—K1 is a good alternative to the text-move.

Beware ! Above all do not play 8. P—Q5, which may lead to the following pretty variation : 8. P—Q5, Kt—K2 ; 9. Kt×P, O—O ; 10. B—B2, P—Q3, and now you must not attempt to make a combination by 11. Kt×P ? since Black will win at once by 11. .... Kt×KBP. The decisive continuations you will be able to find for yourself.

8.	....	O—O

If 8. .... P—Q4, then 9. B×Kt ch, P×B ; 10. Kt—Q4, B—Q2 ; 11. P—B3, Kt—B4 ; 12, P—KB4, and White has a very good game.

9.	Q—Q5	Kt—B4
10.	B—B2	

White has a good game with prospects of a strong attack.

(2) BERLIN DEFENCE

The idea of this defence is to capture White's King's pawn—with the King's Knight—in exchange for Black's. Unfortunately, however, Black cannot maintain his Knight at K5 ; it will be driven away to bad squares and lose much time. This loss of time will have a repercussion on the development of the other pieces with which Black should

immediately occupy himself after his premature attack.
Thus the most active defence actually becomes the most
passive. We may add that the disappearance of the two
King's pawns so simplifies the position that the game loses
much of its interest.

1. P—K4, P—K4 ; 2. Kt—KB3, Kt—QB3 ; 3. B—Kt5,
Kt—B3 ; 4. O—O, Kt×P ; 5. P—Q4, B—K2 ; 6. Q—K2,
Kt—Q3 ; 7. B×Kt, KtP×B ; 8. P×P, Kt—Kt2.

What development is now to be considered for Black ?
If he plays for P—Q4, he will have in his QB4 a very weak
square that White will occupy with a Bishop or a Knight
(B—K3, Kt—QR4, etc.), thus fixing the weak doubled pawns
which will then immediately become a target for White,
e.g., 9. Kt—B3, O—O ; 10. R—K1, Kt—B4 ; 11. Kt—Q4,
Kt—K3 ; 12. B—K3, Kt×Kt; 13. B×Kt, P—Q4; 14. Kt—R4.

Black can improve this variation by first playing P—QB4,
ridding himself of the weakness at his QB4, and then—and
only then—P—Q4, e.g., 13. .... P—QB4 (instead of P—Q4);
14. B—K3, P—Q4 ; 15. P×P, e.p., B×P ; 16. Kt—K4,
B—Kt2 ; 17. Kt×B, P×Kt and, the Bishops being on
different colours, the game seems likely to lead quietly to a
draw, although White maintains the better position. (From
a game of the Tarrasch-Lasker match, Munich, 1908.)

To avoid this equalising variation White must try something else, e.g., 10. Kt—Q4 (instead of R—K1) with the
threat of Kt—B5. If 10. .... Kt—B4, then 11. R—Q1,
Q—K1 ; 12. Kt—B5 with some little attack, or, if 10. ....
B—B4, then 11. R—Q1, B×Kt ; 12. R×B, P—Q4 ; 13. P×P,
e.p., P×P ; 14. P—QKt4 and Black's pawns are weak.

To sum up, we see that in this defence Black can at the
very most hope for a draw, for he has not the slightest
counter-chance. It is for this reason that the Berlin Defence
no longer appears in tournament play.

(3) MORPHY DEFENCE

The variation of the Morphy Defence which we are about
to analyse is similar to the Berlin Defence in that Black makes
use of the attack on White's King's pawn. But here he
delays the capture of that pawn and combines his attack
on it with an action on the Queen's side by which he unpins
his Queen's Knight and succeeds in playing P—Q4 to guard

the Knight when it is at his K5. The game becomes very open but, as always in such cases, to the detriment of Black for the two squares, his K5 and Q4, which he has occupied are weaker in consequence and have to be continually protected.

Moreover, the Knight at K5 cannot be maintained in that advanced post, while White's pawn at K5 has a greater effect than Black's Knight at his K5 and greatly cramps Black's game. White has open lines for an attack and Black, in order to equalise, must have recourse to manœuvres on the Queen's side or in the centre. A very complicated game follows and equilibrium can be maintained only by the utmost care.

The following moves are more or less forced on both sides : 1. P—K4, P—K4 ; 2. Kt—KB3, Kt—QB3 ; 3. B—Kt5, P—QR3 ; 4. B—R4, Kt—B3 ; 5. O—O, Kt×P ; 6. P—Q4, P—QKt4 ; 7. B—Kt3, P—Q4 ; 8. P×P (8. P—QR4 is not any better, Black can reply with 8. .... Kt×QP), B—K3 ; 9. P—B3 (to avoid the exchange of his King's Bishop for Black's Queen's Knight after Kt—R4), B—K2.

We have now arrived at the normal position of this defence.

NO. 9.   POSITION AFTER BLACK'S 9TH MOVE

White has three continuations at his disposal : R—K1, B—K3 and QKt—Q2.

(1) 10.   R—K1

Beware ! This continuation contains a pretty trap, due to Tarrasch, into which Black will fall if, after 10. R—K1, O—O ; 11. Kt—Q4, he plays 11. .... Q—Q2 ?, for White replies with 12. Kt×B, followed by 13. R×Kt, and gains a piece.

But, instead of playing 11. .... Q—Q2 ?, Black can offer a sacrifice of a piece to obtain the attack. It is, perhaps, not absolutely correct but it more or less ensures a draw and even gives some winning chances since it demands of White very exact play. As White, it is safer not to be drawn into this variation.

    10. R—K1, O—O ; 11. Kt—Q4, Kt×KP ; 12. P—B3, B—Q3 ; 13. P×Kt, B—KKt5 ; 14. Q—Q2, Q—R5 ; 15. P—KR3, P—QB4 ; 16. Q—KB2, Q×Q ch ; 17. K×Q, B—Q2, etc.

If White declines the sacrifice and plays, for example, 13. B—KB4 (instead of P×Kt), Black obtains an easy game by 13. .... Kt—B5 ; 14. B×B, Kt(K5)×B. Taking everything into consideration, we can say that White does best to avoid the attack by playing 11. QKt—Q2 (instead of Kt—Q4).

    (2) 10. B—K3

This continuation, which furthers White's development and, above all, protects him against the advance P—Q5, shows at the same time that the position of Black's Knight at K5 is not secure. After 10. .... O—O ; 11. QKt—Q2, the Knight cannot be maintained at K5 since 11. .... P—B4 would compromise Black's game, e.g., 12. P×P, e.p., Kt×P (B3) ; 13. Kt—Kt5 and, however Black replies, White maintains the advantage. If 13. .... B—B2, then 14. Kt×B, R×Kt ; 15. Kt—B3 ; if 13. .... B—KKt5, then 14. P—B3, B—KB4 ; 15. QKt—K4 ; or, if 13. .... Q—Q2, then 14. QKt—K4, QR—Q1 ; 15. Kt×B.

    (3) 10. QKt—Q2

The idea of this move also is to drive away Black's King's Knight. White will attack it a second time by Q—K2, reserving his King's Rook for action on either the Queen's file or the King's Bishop's. The moves QKt—Q2 and Q—K2 can be transposed, for to either Black's best reply is O—O. After these moves the Knight has a good retreat at QB4, where it attacks White's King's Bishop. If the

latter retreats, then 12. .... P—Q5 ! will increase the
mobility of Black's pieces. White must, therefore, parry
this threat and allow the exchange of his King's Bishop.

   10. QKt—Q2, O—O ; 11. Q—K2, Kt—B4 ; 12 Kt—Q4,
Kt×Kt ; 13. P×Kt, Kt×B ; 14. Kt×Kt.

NO. 10.   POSITION AFTER WHITE'S 14TH MOVE

   White has now an open file (the Queen's Bishop's) in
which Black has a backward pawn ; but, if Black succeeds
in playing P—QB4 and P—B5, that pawn will become very
strong. The whole play centres round this threat, which
White must prevent at all costs. If he succeeds, then Black,
in spite of his two Bishops, will have the inferior game.

   In two moves (B—K3 and QR—B1) White can bring
two more pieces to the protection of his QB5 and so prevent
Black's threatened advance. Even by the sacrifice of a
pawn Black cannot succeed in equalising the game, e.g.,
14. .... Q—Q2 ; 15. B—K3, P—QB4 ; 16. P×P, P—Q5 ;
17. KR—Q1. The attack is held up and White is a pawn
ahead. An alternative continuation for White is 17. P—B6
(instead of KR—Q1), Q—B2 ; 18. Kt×P, B—B5 ; 19. Q—Kt4,
B×R ; 20. Kt—B5. He has then for the sacrificed exchange
two pawns and a very strong attack.

   The first of these lines of play is the simplest and surest
way for White to maintain the advantage.

   And now an important remark. If by Kt—B4 followed

by P—Q5 Black can obtain a slight advantage or in any case drawing chances, he must, however, not make this manœuvre too soon and, above all, not before castling. If he does so, White can keep his King's Bishop and remain with the better position.

Let us return to the principal variation and suppose that in reply to 10. QKt—Q2 Black at once plays 10. .... Kt—B4 (instead of O—O). There follows 11. B—B2, P—Q5 ; 12. Kt—K4, P×P ; 13. Kt×Kt, B×Kt ; 14. B—K4, and White has a good game.

The result is even better for White if Black attempts the same manœuvre in the position in the following diagram, arrived at after 1. P—K4, P—K4 ; 2. Kt—KB3, Kt—QB3 ; 3. B—Kt5, P—QR3 ; 4. B—R4, Kt—B3 ; 5. O—O, Kt×P ; 6. P—Q4, P—QKt4 ; 7. B—Kt3, P—Q4 ; 8. P×P, B—K3.

NO. 11. POSITION AFTER BLACK'S 8TH MOVE

9. QKt—Q2, Kt—B4 ; 10. P—B3, P—Q5 ; 11. P×P, Kt×QP ; 12. Kt×Kt, Q×Kt ; 13. B×B, Kt×B ; 14. Q—B3, etc., and White has much the superior position (Capablanca v. Lasker, St. Petersburg Tournament, 1914).

We can then conclude that against any of these active defences White has a continuation to ensure him the superiority. Even if it is not decisive, it explains up to a point why players who are, in general, by no means partial to a passive game have recourse to the passive defences to the Ruy Lopez.

(b) PASSIVE DEFENCES

(1) MORPHY DEFENCE

We have just seen an active variation of the Morphy Defence and now we shall examine a passive one. In the first Black deliberately gave up the centre by allowing the removal of his King's pawn ; in the second, on the contrary, he will maintain it at all costs in order to prepare and to open a counter-offensive on the Queen's side.

This defence to the Ruy Lopez may be considered as one of the safest, for Black's position on the King's side is not weakened at all and he has some chances on the Queen's side. 1. P—K4, P—K4 ; 2. Kt—KB3, Kt—QB3 ; 3. B—Kt5, P—QR3 ; 4. B—R4, Kt—B3 ; 5. O—O, B—K2 (instead of Kt×P, the characteristic move of the active defence) ; 6. R—K1, P—QKt4 ; 7. B—Kt3, P—Q3 ; 8. P—B3.

NO. 12.   POSITION AFTER WHITE'S 8TH MOVE

The object of this move is obvious—the preparation of a retreat for the King's Bishop in reply to Kt—QR4. Nevertheless Black plays 8. .... Kt—QR4 since that move, while threatening to exchange the Knight for the Bishop, allows the liberating move P—B4 to be played immediately. This counter-attack, first suggested by Tchigorin, may be preceded by O—O, B—Kt5, etc., but as a general rule it is better made before White has developed his pieces.

8.	....	Kt—QR4
9.	B—B2	P—B4
10.	P—KR3	

If White reserves this move and plays P—Q4 at once, Black replies with B—Kt5 followed by Kt—B3 with a rather dangerous threat to White's Queen's pawn. In any case, White should play P—KR3 only if he intends to continue with P—Q4 and not P—Q3.

10.	....	Q—B2
11.	P—Q4	O—O
12.	QKt—Q2	Kt—B3

Black can, instead, make one exchange of pawns (BP×P) and then play B—Q2 and KR—B1, but without any advantage. White continues his development with B—Q3, B—K3, etc. If Black makes the exchange before White has played QKt—Q2, that Knight can eventually be played to QB3, which square the exchange of pawns has freed for it.

13. P—Q5

The sacrifice of the Queen's pawn is not quite correct, e.g., 13. Kt—B1, BP×P ; 14. P×P, Kt×QP ; 15 Kt×Kt, P×Kt. If White has not made the "prophylactic" move P—KR3, Black even need not immediately win the pawn but after one exchange of pawns (BP×P) can play B—Kt5 followed, after P—Q5, by Kt—Q5 with a very good game.

| 13. | .... | Kt—Q1 |
| 14. | Kt—B1 | |

(2) STEINITZ DEFENCE

This defence has been preferred by all the champions of the world. It gives a rather difficult game in which Black is very cramped. To explain the preference of the best players for this defence we must—without taking any count of their love of difficulty and complications—remember that White's game is also very difficult and that an error, no matter how slight, may cost him the game. He must be contented with a slow game and must exercise all the more patience since Black's unweakened position presents no target for an attack. The position is full of possibilities which frequently give rise to very subtle position play in which the slightest inexactitude may ruin everything.

The theoretical value of the variations is here of little

importance.   Just as in gambit play, it is the personal qualities
of the artist which play the important part.   In the gambits
it is richness of imagination which decides the issue of the
game ; in this very passive defence to the Ruy Lopez, however, the decisive factor is the sense of position.

The dominating idea in this defence is the non-abandon-
ment of the centre and its defence as long as possible.

1. P—K4, P—K4 ; 2. Kt—KB3, Kt—QB3 ; 3. B—Kt5,
P—Q3 ; 4. P—Q4, Kt—B3 ; 5. O—O, B—Q2 ; 6. R—K1,
B—K2 ; 7. Kt—B3.

NO. 13.   POSITION AFTER WHITE'S 7TH MOVE

The order of these moves, sometimes made too automatically, is of importance. For example, if Black plays
4. .... B—Q2, White, instead of castling, can continue with
5. Kt—B3, *e.g.*, 5. Kt—B3, Kt—B3 ; 6. B×Kt, B×B ;
7. Q—Q3, P×P ; 8. Kt×P and Black is more or less forced
to reply 8. .... B—Q2, followed after 9. B—Kt5, by 9. ....
B—K2, leaving White the choice of transposing into the
main variation (the consideration of which we shall resume
later) by playing 10. O—O or even of playing 10. O—O—O
with a vigorous attack in prospect.

Returning to the position of the last diagram, let us now
look at the "Tarrasch Trap," which needs careful analysis.
In this position Black, having made the most natural developing moves, can apparently continue in the same style and

play 7. .... O—O. If White exchanges Bishop for Knight
(8. B×Kt) in order to win the King's pawn, his own King's
pawn will be attacked by Black's Bishop at QB3 and Knight
at KB3. Moreover, if White exchanges pawns and then
Queens (9. P×P, P×P ; 10. Q×Q), his Rook at K1 will
be unable to leave the back rank (*i.e.*, will not guard the
King's pawn) because of the winning reply R—Q8 ch. *But
Tarrasch's famous trap goes much deeper.*

	7.	O—O ?
	8.	B×Kt	B×B
	9.	P×P	P×P
	10.	Q×Q	QR×Q
	11.	Kt×P	B×P
	12.	Kt×B	Kt×Kt
	13.	Kt—Q3	

   13. R×Kt ?, as mentioned above, is fatal because of the
reply 13. .... R—Q8 ch.

	13.	P—KB4
	14.	P—KB3	B—B4 ch
	15.	Kt×B	

If 15. K—R1, then 15. .... Kt—B7 ch. If, instead,
15. K—B1, then 15. .... B—Kt3, followed, if 16. P×Kt,
by 16. .... P×P ch.

	15.	Kt×Kt
	16.	B—Kt5	R—Q4
	17.	B—K7	R—K1 or B2
	18.	P—QB4	

and White wins the Exchange.

   If at the 10th move Black had taken the Queen with his
King's Rook, the continuation would have been the same with
but this difference—at the 15th move White would play
15. K—B1 for after 15. .... B—Kt3 ; 16. P×Kt, the move
16. .... P×P does not give the discovered check.

   QUESTION 16.   What continuation do you suggest if
Black plays 10. .... B×Q (instead of 10. .... QR×Q) ?
   Let us then avoid Tarrasch's Trap and in the position
of the last diagram decide to play 7. .... P×P. Up to
now Black, playing logically, has developed his game instead
of making this exchange too soon. Now, however, it cannot
be deferred. Black must take.

7. .... P×P (if 7. .... Kt×QP, then 8. Kt×Kt or
first 8. B×B ch); 8. Kt×P, O—O (better than 8. ....
Kt×Kt; 9. Q×Kt, B×B; 10. Kt×B, O—O after which
White gets the advantage by 11. Q—B4); 9. B×Kt, P×B
(in order to keep the two Bishops) and White will develop
his Bishop at either Kt5 or (after P—QKt3) at Kt2. It
must be mentioned that after 8. .... O—O the exchange
9. B×Kt is almost forced. If, for example, White plays
instead 9. Kt—Q5 ?, then 9. .... QKt×Kt; 10. B×B
(otherwise Black will win a piece by B×B), Kt×BP, etc.,
and Black has gained a pawn.

The Steinitz Defence may be preceded by the move
3. .... P—QR3, i.e., 3. .... P—QR3 ; 4. B—R4 and now
4. .... P—Q3. But White can with advantage enter upon
the ordinary variation by 5. B×Kt ch, P×B ; 6. P—Q4,
P×P ; 7. Kt×P, B—Q2 for the position of Black's pawn
at QR3 (instead of QR2) has its drawbacks.

Finally, let us mention another trap, which can, however,
easily be avoided. If after 1. P—K4, P—K4 ; 2. Kt—KB3,
Kt—QB3 ; 3. B—Kt5, P—QR3 ; 4. B—R4, P—Q3 White
plays at once, 5. P—Q4, Black replies thus : 5. .... P—QKt4 ;
6. B—Kt3, Kt×P ; 7. Kt×Kt, P×Kt, whereupon 8. Q×P ?
would lose a piece, e.g., 8. .... P—QB4 ; 9. Q—Q5, B—K3 ;
10. Q—B6 ch, B—Q2 ; 11. Q—Q5, P—B5 ! White must
first play 8. B—Q5 and then (after 8. .... R—Kt1) 9. Q×P.
Similarly, if 6. .... P×P, then 7. B—Q5 !, B—Q2 ; 8. Kt×P.

THE SIESTA GAMBIT

We have just seen that after 1. P—K4, P—K4 ; 2. Kt—KB3,
Kt—QB3 ; 3. B—Kt5, P—QR3 ; 4. B—R4, P—Q3 White
is more or less forced to continue with either 5. B×Kt ch
or 5. P—Q4. Among inferior continuations at White's
disposal there is one (5. P—B3) which gives Black the opportunity of seizing the initiative in real gambit style. (This
line is known as the Siesta Gambit and has been much played
in recent years).

The move 5. P—B3 (played in order to recapture at Q4
with this pawn) contains no direct threat and this fact allows
Black to free his game by an enterprising move, which we
have not yet met in the Ruy Lopez, 5. .... P—B4. This
enterprising, almost risky, move weakens Black's King's side

in alarming fashion. Nevertheless, an attempt by White to rush the attack seems to lead to a draw, *e.g.*, 6. P—Q4, BP×P ; 7. Kt×P, P×Kt ; 8. Q—R5 ch, K—K2 ; 9. B—Kt 5 ch, Kt—B3 ; 10. KB×Kt, P×B ; 11. P×P, Q—Q4 ; 12. B—R4, K—K3 ; 13. B×Kt, P×B, 14. Q—K8 ch, K—B4 ; 15. Q—R5 ch, with perpetual check.

White, it is true, has a better continuation : 6. P×P, B×P ; 7. P—Q4, P—K5 ; 8. Kt—Kt5 (if 8. B—KKt5, then 8. .... B—K2 ; 9. Kt—R4, B—K3), Kt—B3 ; 9. P—B3, P×P ; 10. O—O with a strong attack. 10. Q×P gives nothing, *e.g.*, 10. .... Q—K2 ch ; 11. K—B1, B—Kt5 ; 12. B×Kt ch, K—Q1, etc.

QUESTION 17. In the variation arising from 6. P×P, cannot Black's play be strengthened by 8. .... P—Q4 (instead of 8. .... Kt—B3) ?

FOUR KNIGHTS' GAME

(1. P—K4, P—K4 ; 2. KT—KB3, KT—QB3 ; 3. KT—B3, KT—B3)

The Four Knights' Game is one of the quietest. White temporarily renounces the initiative and strives above all for the development of his pieces. Thus, move after move, the position is for a long time in equilibrium, and is sometimes even symmetrical since Black merely copies his opponent's moves. For example, 1. P—K4, P—K4 ; 2. Kt—KB3, Kt—QB3 ; 3. Kt—B3, Kt—B3 ; 4. B—Kt5, B—Kt5 ; 5. O—O, O—O ; 6. P—Q3, P—Q3.

It is possible to continue in this style for some moves further, *e.g.*, 7. Kt—K2, Kt—K2 ; 8. Kt—Kt3, Kt—Kt3, etc.

But Black may fall into the mistake of believing that he can unthinkingly continue to repeat White's moves. But as soon as White makes a slightly aggressive move, Black must abandon the symmetry or he will automatically suffer disaster. Going back to the position after Black's 6th move, for example, let us suppose that he continues to imitate his opponent. Here is a continuation in which he can speedily be mated, even if White does not always make the best moves :—

7. B—Kt5, B—Kt5 ; 8. Kt—Q5, Kt—Q5 ; 9. Kt×B, Kt×B ; 10. Kt—Q5, Kt—Q5 ; 11. Kt×Kt ch, P×Kt ;

12. B—R6, Kt×Kt ch ; 13. P×Kt, B—R6 ; 14. K—R1,
K—R1 ; 15. B×R, B×R ; 16. B—R6, B—R6 ; 17. Q—Q2,
Q—Q2 ; 18. R—KKt1, R—KKt1 ; 19. R×R ch, K×R ;
20, Q—K1, followed by 21. Q—Kt1 ch and Q—Kt7 mate.

It is thus at the 7th move that Black should change his
line of play, at the moment when White, having just pinned
the King's Knight, threatens to reinforce the attack on that
piece by playing Kt—Q5 :—

7. B—Kt5, B×Kt ; 8. P×B, Q—K2 ; 9. R—K1, Kt—Q1 ;
10. P—Q4, Kt—K3 ; 11. B—QB1, P—B3 ; 12. B—B1,
Q—B2, etc.

Black's excellent development has enabled him to repulse
without difficulty an attack carried out by as many pieces
as could be mustered for the defence.

Besides it is only logical that, if White does not seize the
initiative in the opening in order to increase his advantage,
he will be forced to wait till the middle-game for the opportunity to recur.

White's tame play in this opening may even incite Black
to a more active game from the very beginning. He can,
for example, renounce the quiet move P—Q3 and bravely
try P—Q4. Admittedly, this move is rather bold and leads
to a somewhat dangerous position for Black, a fact that will
not astonish us :—

6. P—Q3, B×Kt ; 7. P×B, P—Q4 ; 8. B×Kt, P×B ;
9. Kt×P, Q—Q3 ; 10. B—B4, R—K1; 11. Q—B3 (if 11. P×P,
then 11. .... R×Kt ; 12. P—Q4, R—K8 !), P×P ; 12. P×P,
R×Kt ; 13. R—Q1 with approximate equality.

QUESTION 18. Which Rook should White play to Q1 at
the 13th move in this variation ? Note that in this position
there is a pretty trap and that there are good reasons for
choosing one Rook rather than the other.

Black can even try to take the initiative as early as the 4th
move. Obviously he must expect some difficulties but, at
least, the doubtful fight that follows will force White out of
his apathy and perhaps teach him a lesson.

After 1. P—K4, P—K4 ; 2. Kt—KB3, Kt—QB3 ; 3. Kt—B3
Kt—B3, the Knights' moves have led to a symmetrical position, White's 3rd move having annulled the advantage of
his 2nd. Black takes advantage of this and is no longer
content to copy his opponent by replying to 4. B—Kt5 with

4. .... B—Kt5. Instead, he makes the attacking move, 4. .... Kt—Q5. This is a gambit—Rubinstein's—since the King's pawn is *en prise*.

5. Kt×P, Kt×KP; 6. Kt×Kt, Kt×B; 7. Kt×BP, Q—K2; 8. Kt×R, Q×Kt ch; 9. K—B1, Kt—Q5; 10. P—Q3, etc. Or 5. Kt×P, Q—K2; 6. P—B4, Kt×B; 7. Kt×Kt, P—Q3; 8. Kt—KB3, Q×P ch; 9. K—B2, Kt—Kt5 ch; 10. K—Kt3, Q—Kt3; 11. Kt—R4, Q—R4; 12. P—KR3, etc.

We see to what extravagant variations this gambit leads. Actually, White should accept it and boldly face the dangers of that enterprise for, though he has momentarily lost the initiative, he may hope to recapture it later. If, however, after choosing so quiet an opening, he finds a difficulty in suddenly embarking on such extraordinary adventures, he can choose a quieter continuation in reply to Black's gambit, *e.g.*, 5. O—O, 5. B—R4, 5. B—B4 or even 5. Kt×Kt.

QUESTION 19. Who has the advantage in the two variations of Rubinstein's gambit that we have given ? Suggest possible continuations.

KING'S GAMBIT

(1. P—K4, P—K4 ; 2. P—KB4)

In the opinion of many amateurs, the most vulnerable point in the original position is KB2, and even after castling it does not seem to be entirely unassailable for the Rook cannot stay at KB1 indefinitely.

Those amateurs appeal to practical experience in support of their opinion. Of course, it cannot be denied that attacks on this pawn have succeeded time and again, particularly as this pawn is undefended for a long while in the opening and serves as a target for the adversary. It requires only a slight mistake and it will be lost, and with its fall the whole game collapses. Have we not seen that, in the Giuoco Piano, Evans Gambit, Two Knights' Defence and the Hanham Defence, White hurriedly brings out his pieces for an immediate attack on Black's King's Bishop's pawn, an attack which Black can only repel with difficulty ? Of course one should always be able to find a satisfactory defence against a premature assault like this ; on the other hand how often does one not fall with one's eyes open into a trap based on the weakness of this pawn ? By way of example we give here one of the most famous, the celebrated "Légal's Mate," known for over a century.

Beware !   A trap.

1. P—K4, P—K4 ; 2. Kt—KB3, Kt—QB3 ; 3. B—B4, P—KR3 ; 4. P—Q4, P—Q3 ; 5. Kt—B3, B—Kt5 ; 6. P×P, Kt×P ; 7. Kt×Kt !, B×Q ; 8. B×P ch, K—K2 ; 9. Kt—Q5 mate.

Observe that this mate would not be possible if Black's King's Knight were at B3, or if White's Queen's Knight had not moved to B3, or after other moves ; this makes this mate exceptional.

From the modern point of view, all premature attacks, made before the pieces are developed, ought to be repulsed, and the attack on the King's Bishop's pawn should be no exception, although its defence may sometimes be difficult and require to be carried out with circumspection.   Actually its weakness gives the attacker many chances and hence arises the idea of opening the King's Bishop's file to strengthen the attack.

We thus come to the King's Gambit in which White's second move is P—KB4, sacrificing the pawn for the immediate opening of the King's Bishop's file.   But this is not the sole object of the sacrifice : actually it is an attack against Black's castled position which is being prepared.

Further—and perhaps this is most important—by drawing Black's King's pawn away from the centre, White is free to play P—Q4.   To strengthen his centre, often with a gain of time, White employs his King's Bishop's pawn, which usually takes no part in the battle for the centre.   We recall here that in the Evans Gambit a pawn on the flank is sacrificed to allow White to play P—Q4 without loss of time. In virtue of the importance of the centre in the openings, one should always attempt to lure the opposing pieces and pawns towards the wings.

Of course, the advance P—KB4 is not without danger to White himself, for it enormously weakens his own castled position so that Black can speculate on this weakness and, without accepting the gambit, play B—B4.   Avoiding the complications of combinations with a pawn to the good, Black contents himself with sound and solid positional play in which White has not to think only of the safety of his castled position, but has even to run the risk of not being able to castle.

The move P—KB4 has yet another disadvantage for White, for it allows Black the move P—Q4, which is so important in the open games. The move P—Q4 is in accordance with the general principle that an advance on the flank should be met with an advance in the centre and this principle is justified more than ever in this opening for P—Q4 facilitates for Black the development of his pieces, while the move P—KB4 does not serve the same purpose for White. However, the premature advance P—Q4, as we have often observed, always entails some risk; here Black plays, in effect, a sort of counter-gambit by himself giving up a pawn, and, as in the Two Knights' Defence, his boldness leads to an unsound position.

If, on the other hand, Black accepts the gambit, he has two lines of defence. He may either seek to develop his pieces as quickly as possible, according to sound principles, and not worry too much about maintaining his pawn advantage or, on the contrary, he may defend his pawn at all costs not only to remain materially stronger, but also to use this pawn as his best protection against an attack along the King's Bishop's file. In this case, White's attack will become very strong, and should permit of fresh sacrifices, even of pieces, to break down the resistance of his opponent, and to arrive at length at the opening of the King's Bishop's file.

However, it must not be thought that only a sudden attack, with sacrifices and brilliant combinations, can bring White victory. On the contrary, his superior development, completed before that of his opponent, allows him to follow a quiet line of play, almost a positional game, and there are abundant examples in which White, even by exchanging Queens, obtains a superior and even winning position. As for brilliant combinations, it is not rare to see them break down against Black's resistance, after sacrifices too numerous and heavy for White to bear.

That is why the majority of the older gambits are of little use to us, and as they are scarcely ever played nowadays, it is better for us only to give the simpler lines of play both for Black and for White.

We shall first examine the gambit declined, and afterwards

the gambit accepted. The latter divides itself into two sections : (a) the King's Knight's Gambit and (b) the King's Bishop's Gambit. This distinction has point only when Black wants to hold on to his pawn.

(a) KING'S GAMBIT DECLINED

1.	P—K4	P—K4
2.	P—KB4	B—B4

It would be a gross error to play 2. .... P—Q3 here as many inexperienced amateurs do. Once you decide not to take the pawn, you should at least profit by the weakness that P—KB4 will create in White's castled position; if you do not, you lessen your own chances because you leave to White all the advantages of this premature advance without taking advantage of the risks attending it. White will have the advantage in the centre with three pawns against two, a comfortable castled position, and all his pieces will come out rapidly, while Black would have a cramped game with his King's Bishop shut in, and not even a good centre. As for the Bishop's file, White can always open it when he likes.

3. Kt—KB3

Obviously, White cannot play 3. P×P on account of 3. .... Q—R5 ch; 4. P—Kt3, Q×KP ch, followed by 5. .... Q×R. This manœuvre is too simple to be classed as a trap; it is merely a blunder on White's part.

3.	....	P—Q3
4.	Kt—B3	

Practically the same variations occur after 4. B—B4. By 4. P—B3, which seems more promising, White temporarily abandons the rapid development of his pieces to reinforce the centre with a fourth pawn. Black's best reply to this move is 4. .... B—Kt3, with the continuation 5. P—Q4 (if 5. BP×P, then 5. .... QP×P), Kt—KB3. Black may, however, attempt to play a sort of "Siesta Gambit" by 4. .... P—KB4.

NO. 14. POSITION AFTER 4. .... P—KB4

in the note to White's 4th move

This position leads to extremely interesting and complicated variations, *e.g.*

    5. BP×P   QP×P

The same variations may occur in the Soldatenkoff Attack in which White plays first 4. BP×P and, after 4. .... QP×P, then 5. P—B3. But to that attack Black can reply with 5. .... Kt—KB3 instead of 5. .... P—KB4

    6. P—Q4   KP×P

    7. B—QB4   BP×P

    8. Kt—K5

and one's brain would reel under the analysis of all the possible continuations.

QUESTION 20. How would you continue the variation after 4. P—B3, B—Kt3 ; 5. P×P, P×P ; 6. Kt×P ? (See note to White's 4th move.)

Let us now return to the main variation (1. P—K4, P—K4 ; 2. P—KB4, B—B4 ; 3. Kt—KB3, P—Q3 ; 4. Kt—B3)

    4. ....   Kt—KB3

    5. B—B4   Kt—B3

    6. P—Q3

This position is typical of the King's Gambit Declined. It may be reached by a different order of moves and may be derived from other openings, *e.g.*, the Vienna Game.

NO. 15. POSITION AFTER WHITE'S 6TH MOVE.

White here has some difficulty in castling; to do so he must play either Kt—QR4 or else Q—K2 followed by B—K3. On the other hand, he has some attacking chances, for he threatens, after exchanging pawns, to play B—KKt5 and Kt—Q5.

    6. ....   B—KKt5

Black may play instead 6. .... B—K3 (which, however, complicates the game by creating weaknesses in the centre) or even 6. .... P—QR3.

    7. P—KR3

The move 7. Kt—QR4 would, perhaps, be stronger.

    7. ....   B×Kt
    8. Q×B   P×P

Better than 8. .... Kt—Q5 immediately, which would give White a strong attack as follows: 8. .... Kt—Q5; 9. Q—Kt3, Kt×P ch; 10. K—Q1, Kt×R; 11. Q×P, K—Q2; 12. P×P, P×P; 13. R—B1, etc. Black can avoid all these complications by playing simply 8. .... Q—K2 and castling (QR), although in this case, too, White obtains a strong attack.

    9. B×P   Kt—Q5
    10. Q—Kt3   Kt—R4
    11. Q—Kt4   Kt×B
    12. Q×Kt   Kt×P ch
    13. K—Q1   Kt—K6 ch

Although Black has still some difficulties to surmount, he has emerged safely from the complications of the opening.

(b) FALKBEER COUNTER-GAMBIT

1.	P—K4	P—K4
2.	P—KB4	P—Q4

A sound idea, but it demands sacrifices for its object to be realised.

3. KP×P

To avoid the dangers of this gambit, White can decline the sacrifice—by 3. Kt—KB3, QP×P ; 4. Kt×P. But then he can reckon on no advantage after 4. .... Kt—Q2 and the advance of his King's Bishop's pawn has no longer any force or meaning.

3. ....   P—K5

3. .... Q×P would cause Black to lose several important tempi. On the other hand 3. .... P—QB3 would give him a flexible and not very dangerous game, e.g., 4. Kt—QB3, KP×P (if 4. .... BP×P ; 5. P×P, P—Q5 ; 6. Kt—K4, Q—Q4 ; 7 B—Q3) ; 5. Kt—B3, Kt—B3 ; 6 P—Q4, etc.

QUESTION 21. Why cannot 4. QP×P, Kt×P ; 5. P×P be played in that variation ?

4. P—Q3

There are several ways of continuing here, such as the older move 4. B—Kt5 ch ; we give here the safest.

4.	....	Kt—KB3
5.	P×P	Kt×KP
6.	Kt—KB3	

After 6. Q—K2, 6. .... Q×P gives Black a satisfactory game.

6.	....	B—QB4
7.	Q—K2	B—B4

7. .... B—B7, ch would lose immediately—by 8. K—Q1, Q×P ch ; 9. KKt—Q2 !, P—KB4 ; 10. Kt—B3, etc.

NO. 16.   POSITION AFTER BLACK'S 7TH MOVE

A position to remember. It will well repay study.

8. Kt—B3

Beware ! The gain of a piece by 8. P—KKt4 would be bad. Black would reply with 8. .... O—O; 9. P×B, R—K1 and have a winning attack.

8. ....   Q—K2

Here 8. .... O—O would not be the correct move on account of 9. Kt×Kt, R—K1 ; 10. Kt—K5.

9. B—K3

Other moves give no better results owing to the threat of 9.... B—B7 ch.

9.	....	B×B
10.	Q×B	Kt×Kt
11.	Q×Q ch	K×Q
12.	P×Kt	B—K5
13.	P—B4	P—QB3
14.	P×P	B×Kt
15.	P—B7	Kt—B3
16.	P×B	

with an even game.

(c) KING'S GAMBIT ACCEPTED
(1) KING'S KNIGHT'S GAMBIT

1.	P—K4	P—K4
2.	P—KB4	P×P
3.	Kt—KB3	P—Q4

You see that even in a gambit this move, like all those which tend to command the centre and facilitate the development of the pieces, is possible, and often provides the best means of defence, because it opposes a sound line of play to the somewhat adventurous game of your opponent. However, Black can, instead, play 3. .... P—KKt4, to defend and keep the pawn after the capture. These pawns, forming a defensive chain, may even become a weapon for attacking the weakened castled position of the enemy and exerting a strong and continuous pressure on his position. White, on his part, must endeavour to break down this barrier, either by 4. B—B4 or 4. P—KR4, even at the cost of heavy sacrifices.

4.	P×P	Kt—KB3
5.	Kt—B3	Kt×P
6.	Kt×Kt	Q×Kt
7.	P—Q4	B—K2
8.	P—B4	Q—Q3

A position offering equal chances.

(2) KING'S BISHOP'S GAMBIT

1.	P—K4	P—K4
2.	P—KB4	P×P
3.	B—B4	Kt—KB3

Here also 3. .... P—Q4 would provide an adequate defence. If instead of playing either 3. .... P—Q4 or the text-move, Black wishes to defend his pawn at B5, he should play 3. .... Q—R5 ch, and after 4. K—B1, P—KKt4 ; the position would become very complicated.

4.	Kt—QB3	P—B3

In preparation for the advance of the Queen's Knight's pawn to Kt4 and Kt5, which would win the weak King's pawn. White's best reply appears to be 5. B—Kt3.

5.	Q—B3	

5. P—Q4 would be a mistake for 5. .... B—Kt5 ! would carry with it a very disagreeable threat in 6. .... P—Q4.

5.	....	P—Q4

5. .... Q—K2 would be bad because of 6. KKt—K2, after which 6. .... P—QKt4 would lose—by 7. B×P, P×B ; 8. P—K5.

	6.	P×P	B—Q3
	7.	P—Q4	B—KKt5
	8.	Q—B2	O—O
	9.	B×P	P×P

Or first 9. .... R—K1 ch ; 10. K—B1.

	10.	B×P	Kt×B
	11.	Kt×Kt	Q—R4 ch
	12.	Kt—B3	B—Kt5
	13.	B—Q2	R—K1 ch
	14.	K—B1	Kt—B3

It is now Black who has the attack and superior development.

QUESTION 22. Can you give a variation of the King's Bishop's Gambit in which Black defends his pawn at B5 ?

SECOND GROUP

CLOSE GAMES

(1. P—Q4, P—Q4)

With the close openings, which are generally characterised by the move 1. P—Q4, we enter quite a new field which has practically nothing in common with the open games we have just analysed, and which, on the other hand, embraces nearly all the other openings we have yet to see. There is, in fact, a striking resemblance between the close openings and all the others (with the exception of the open games), to such an extent that one can almost divide the entire range of openings into two main groups: (a) The open games, (b) the others.

By the "close games," which we are about to study we mean the Queen's Pawn Game and Gambit (1. P—Q4, P—Q4). We shall devote a little space to the Dutch Defence (1. P—Q4, P—KB4). For the time being, however, we shall confine our attention to the Queen's Pawn Game and Gambit, and postpone the explanation of the peculiarities of the Dutch Defence.

Right at the beginning, the study of the Queen's Pawn Game confronts us with one great difficulty. The generic term (Queen's Pawn Game) is applied to quite a number of varied openings which have to be studied separately. It is just as if, in the open games, no distinction was made between the Ruy Lopez, Giuoco Piano, etc. Under the heading of "Queen's Pawn Game" we discuss different attacks and defences, etc., which might well be called by distinctive names.

At first sight, casual observers might claim that the difference between the Open Games (1. P—K4, P—K4) and the Close Games (1. P—Q4, P—Q4) is not nearly so great as it appears, because in both groups the constituent moves tend towards the occupation of the centre. The Open Games have in view the advance P—Q4, just as the Close Games envisage the move P—K4 (either in one stage or in two). The

difference is, however, so great that the two lines of play
and even the two systems of reasoning do not resemble
each other in the slightest.

We have already said that the Open Games are based on
two King-centres, while the Close Games are the result of
a struggle between two Queen-centres. This means that in
the latter type, the idea of an immediate attack on the King's
position is abandoned, and White contents himself with a
slower game giving slight advantages in the centre and on
the Queen's side. Brilliant combinations and fierce attacks
against the King are not entirely excluded from these openings, but they are held back until later. At first it is a
question of building up a strong position which will allow
these manœuvres to take place.

The Queen-centre is more solid than the King-centre for
the simple reason that the Queen's pawn is defended by the
Queen and will only become weak if it is isolated. And yet,
how often does this pawn, even when isolated, become a
strong weapon in itself or as a support for pieces occupying
K5 and QB5 ! But there is another reason, very much more
important. It lies in the fact that the Queen-centre can be
formed with three pawns, while the King-centre consists of
only two—for the King's Bishop's pawn, by advancing, creates
too great a weakness in the castled position to be of service
in the battle for the centre—and even then one of these
pawns may be rapidly exchanged.

On the other hand, the Queen's Bishop's pawn can, with
a Queen-centre, be advanced very early without any danger,
either to protect the centre (P—QB3) or to attack the hostile
centre (P—QB4). If one of the three pawns is exchanged,
there will still be two in the centre, and when these are the
King's and Queen's pawns, they form in the centre a very
tower of strength which it will not be easy to destroy.

This already gives us a piece of valuable information. In
order to preserve the balance of the game, it is essential that
both players shall have free movement of their Queen's
Bishop's pawns to make them take part in the struggle for
the centre at the opportune moment ; it is therefore very
important not to obstruct their advance. It is obvious that
if our opponent has three pawns (QBP, QP, KP) at his
disposal on the principal part of the board against two of

ours (QP and KP) our position there will gradually become untenable ; and it is above all to Black that this remark is addressed, for many amateurs have a tendency to play 2. .... Kt—QB3 after 1. P—Q4, P—Q4 ; 2. P—QB4. I do not go so far as to say that this move involves the loss of the game ; it is, in fact, one of the constituent moves of Tchigorin's Defence, but this defence is an exception to the general rule which we must first investigate thoroughly. When we thoroughly understand the essential principles of the Close Games, we shall have the right to take liberties, but not before. There are other good reasons for considering the move Kt—QB3, played before the advance of the Queen's Bishop's pawn, as bad both for White and for Black. Let us consider it from Black's point of view. After White has played P—QB4 there is always the possibility that he will open the Queen's Bishop's file along which his Rook will exert a strong pressure ; the pawn at Black's QB2 will be constantly threatened and the Knight at his QB3 will be pinned. White can strengthen his attack by playing a Bishop to KB4 and a Knight to QKt5—and already we see to what defensive manœuvres Black will be reduced to give free movement to his unfortunate Knight ! Therefore, bear this well in mind—in the Queen's Pawn Game never play your Queen's Knight in front of your Queen's Bishop's pawn. First play P—QB4 and then, and only then, Kt—QB3.

It is the solidity of the centre, based on the three pawns there and the fact that the Queen's pawn is defended, which gives the "close" character to these openings. It is also the reason why the threats are not so direct as in the open game. It is not at all a question of obtaining an obvious advantage in the opening but rather of preparing a sequence of subtle and long-range manœuvres. It is real position play, depending on the possibility of strong and weak squares. One tries to create weaknesses in one's opponent's position while avoiding them in one's own. One seeks to occupy important squares while reducing one's opponent to the defensive on inferior or weakened ones.

To be able to play the close openings well we must first grasp the elementary ideas of positional play and more particularly the idea of "strong" and "weak" squares. We must first learn the definition of strong and weak squares and how they are recognised : we must further know how to create or avoid weaknesses, how to attack weakened squares and finally what pieces we should keep in order to profit by a weakness or nullify its effects. Thus we have a new science which found no application in the study of the open games.

We cannot, indeed, stop to explain this science in detail here : its place is in the general theory of the game. But in order to make our explanation of the close games understandable, we shall first of all make a rapid survey of the essential ideas concerning weakness on the board.

WEAKNESSES ON THE CHESSBOARD

Steinitz first pointed out the existence of "holes" in a position. The square QKt3, if the pawns are at QR3, QKt2 and QB3, is a case in point. It is not the most characteristic example of this kind of weakness but it is the most obvious and best known. Nevertheless, we can deduce from it the simplest definition of a weak square ; *it is a square which is not defended by a pawn.* If, however, this square can be subsequently defended by a pawn, its temporary weakness is often quite insignificant. The defending pawn can sometimes be advantageously replaced by a piece for that purpose : in the Fianchetto it is a Bishop which performs the task. As long as a Bishop remains at Kt2 the squares B3 and R3, weakened by the advance of the Knight's pawn, are sufficiently guarded. However, the Bishop will not remain indefinitely at Kt2 for it is an active piece and not a defensive pawn. From the moment it is moved or exchanged (and this is a new type of threat) the weakness of the squares B3 and R3 is manifest. So squares like pieces cannot be better defended than by pawns. Further, we should train ourselves to disregard the pieces in order to study the position of the pawns themselves, or what we might call the pawn-skeleton. It is thus that we shall succeed in distinguishing strong squares from weak in our own position as well as in our opponent's.

The importance of a pawn as a defensive weapon is seen not only in positions containing pieces but even on an almost empty board. For example, place a White Knight and a

Black Knight each at Q4 : one is as strong as the other. But it is sufficient to add only a pawn to make their values change : the Knight which is supported by a pawn at K3 will be much stronger than the unsupported Knight. Q4 becomes then a strong square from which the former cannot be dislodged, while the latter will have to move at the approach of the enemy King.

If we add a White Bishop and a Black Bishop, the strongest positions of each Knight will be on a square of the opposite colour to that on which the hostile Bishop stands (here the Bishop partially replaces a pawn). We may conclude from this that the value of a square does not only depend on the position of the pawns but also on the presence of one piece or another. To have a "weak square" is not necessarily synonymous with having a "weakness," if there are no pieces to take advantage of it or if we have a piece to protect it. Similarly a strong square is quite useless if we have no piece to profit by it. On the other hand, a piece posted on a strong square and supported by a pawn, becomes so powerful that a lost game may be drawn or a draw turned into a win by it. Dr. Tarrasch has rightly said that a Knight in the centre, supported by a pawn, has the power of a Rook. Here are some examples to illustrate the truth of this remark.

NO. 17.   CAPABLANCA *v.* ALEKHINE

In spite of being a pawn down, Black drew the game,

thanks to his Knight posted on a White square in the centre
and supported by a pawn.   It was stronger than the hostile
Bishop.

NO. 18.   LASKER *v.* JANOWSKI

Though Black was the Exchange down, he won the game
by virtue of his centrally-posted Knight supported by a pawn.

NO. 19.   ALLIES *v.* ZNOSKO-BOROVSKY
(Toulouse, 1930)

Black won; his Knight was better posted than his
opponents' because it could neither be attacked by the
Bishop nor dislodged by a pawn.

A weak square for one player will become a strong square for his opponent if he can place a suitable piece on it and keep it there. A momentary occupation alone is not much use ; and once again we look to the pawns to make the occupation of a strong square a lasting one. Thus it is the pawns which make strong and weak squares, but the strength of a square is also influenced by pieces.

Although a piece cannot be driven away from a strong square except by a pawn, it runs the risk, however, of being exchanged for a hostile piece. Then comes the question of deciding whether the recapture should be made by a pawn or by another piece. The answer depends on circumstances ; nevertheless the following rule will help us : If it is a question of occupying the strong square, take back with a piece ; recapture with a pawn only when, by so doing, you obtain a strongly-defended passed pawn. It is not advantageous to recapture with a pawn, if, on the same file in front of the occupied square, there is a hostile backward pawn, because the file should then remain open for an attack on that backward pawn.

NO. 20.   WHITE HAS A STRONG SQUARE AT QB5 AND BLACK
A BACKWARD PAWN AT QB2

The position arises in the following manner : (Ruy Lopez)
1. P—K4, P—K4 ; 2. Kt—KB3, Kt—QB3 ; 3. B—Kt5,
P—QR3 ; 4. B—R4, Kt—B3 ; 5. O—O, Kt×P ; 6. P—Q4,

P—QKt4 ; 7. B—Kt3, P—Q4 ; 8. P×P, B—K3 ; 9. P—B3,
B—K2 ; 10. QKt—Q2, O—O ; 11. Q—K2, Kt—B4 ;
12. Kt—Q4, Kt×Kt ; 13. P×Kt, Kt×B ; 14. Kt×Kt.

In the above diagram not only has White a strong square
at QB5, but Black has a weak one at QB3 and, above all, a
weak pawn at QB2. By posting his Knight at QB5 White
not only occupies this strong square but he "fixes" the two
weaknesses of his opponent. Thus our first care on noticing
a weakness in the hostile position should be to prevent the
enemy from getting rid of it.

To attain this end, we must either place a piece in front
of the square occupied by the pawn or else threaten the
square which the weak pawn would occupy by moving.

In the foregoing position, for example, Black would get
rid of his weak pawn at QB2 by advancing it to QB4 ; if it
reached QB5 it would even become very strong. Hence
Black's weakness at QB2 should be "fixed" by posting the
Knight on QB5, always with the proviso that, if the Knight
is exchanged, the recapture can be made with a piece, for,
by taking back with a pawn, the weakness is allowed to
disappear.

**NO 21.   BLACK HAS A WEAK SQUARE AT HIS QB4—A STRONG
SQUARE FOR WHITE.**

The position is reached in the Tarrasch Defence to the
Queen's Gambit :—1. P—Q4, P—Q4 ; 2. P—QB4, P—K3 ;

3. Kt—QB3, P—QB4 ; 4. BP×P, KP×P ; 5. Kt—B3, Kt—QB3 ; 6. P—KKt3, Kt—B3 ; 7. B—Kt2, B—K2 ; 8. O—O, O—O ; 9. P×P, B×P ; 10. Kt—QR4, B—K2 ; 11. B—K3.

Here it might be maintained that the capture by a pawn at QB5 would fix Black with a weak pawn at QKt2, but it must not be forgotten that White's pawn at QB5 would be isolated and easily attacked. To sum up, it is always preferable to adhere to the recapture by a piece in similar cases. The piece will play an active part; if a pawn, posted on a strong square, happens to have just as active a role (*e.g.*, at K5), there is then no objection whatever in preferring the recapture with the pawn.

Thus before occupying strong squares (or our opponent's weak squares) we must "observe" them ; that is to say we must bring the required number of pieces to threaten the square or squares in front of them. The weak square or pawn is thus "fixed" and the strong square is occupied at the proper moment when the piece in occupation will not be dislodged or exchanged with advantage.

NO. 22. NIMZOWITSCH v. SALVE

(Carlsbad Tournament, 1911)

The three White pieces, Queen, Bishop and Knight—to which will be added a fourth, the Queen's Rook (when it moves to K1)—defend the square K5 and keep back Black's

weak pawn at K3.   An example of control instead of
occupation.

Evidently the preceding remarks, advising you to mass as
many pieces as possible on one point, appear to offend
against the rule of economy of force which requires one
piece to protect several points.   However, this anxious desire
for economy must not be pushed to excess, for too much work
for one piece would not be well done.   Also, when it is a
question of a "critical" square where the fate of the battle
is decided, no piece is superfluous.   It would be criminal
folly to resolve to ignore these critical squares which are the
key to the position.   We shall make the affirmation many
times in the modern openings, in which, from the very beginning, the game is played around these squares ; plausible
moves are not sufficient if they do not subscribe to the
strategical object of the opening.

In short, the question of weak squares has led us to the
discovery of the strategical plan.

In chess, as in art, every detail counts.

QUEEN'S PAWN GAME AND QUEEN'S GAMBIT

(1. P—Q4, P—Q4)

This preamble will now be of service to us in establishing
the particular tendencies of the close openings as compared
with those of the open games ; the hand-to-hand struggle
is avoided, the battle is joined on the Queen's side, where
the operations have not the keenness of King's side operations, the weakening manœuvres proceed slowly with the
maximum of security.

Instead of the clash of pieces in the open games, we have
here the slow creation of points of support for pieces and
pawns.

We can already see the difference in spirit and easily understand why we cannot play the close games in the manner
of the open ones without showing a gross lack of appreciation.

Let us now analyse, as closely as possible, the peculiarities
of the Queen's Pawn Game.

We have seen that in the close games the centre is firmer
than in the open game thanks to the three pawns forming it,

and that the Queen's Bishop's pawn must retain the option of advancing one or two squares. But as Black's Queen's pawn will be attacked after 1. P—Q4, P—Q4 ; 2. P—QB4 by 3. Kt—QB3, he must defend it first, obviously by P—K3, before allowing himself to play P—QB4. We thus arrive at a configuration recalling the Philidor Defence (1. P—K4, P—K4 ; 2. Kt—KB3, P—Q3) or the Ruy Lopez (1. P—K4, P—K4 ; 2. Kt—KB3, Kt—QB3 ; 3. B—Kt5, P—Q3) with the same consequences : one of the Black Bishops cannot be developed. It is therefore of importance to determine clearly first of all whether the Queen's Bishop should be developed before P—K3 by playing, say, B—KB4.

Black's Queen's Bishop in leaving the Queen's side weakens it perceptibly, for it is on this flank, as we already know, that the struggle will begin. The Black pawn at Q4 is not sufficiently defended and the QKtP will be undefended ; and these facts will allow White to begin a direct attack, *e.g.*, 1. P—Q4, P—Q4 ; 2. P—QB4, B—B4 ; 3. Q—Kt3, and White wins a pawn. This type of threat is always present in this opening because of the advance of the Queen's Bishop's pawn. Therefore Black must always ask himself, before moving the Queen's Bishop, how he will protect his Queen's Knight's pawn.

Moves of the Queen (Q—B1, Q—B2 and Q—Q2) do not give complete satisfaction. In the first case the Queen hampers the movements of the Queen's Rook ; in the second she is posted on the Queen's Bishop's file which is always likely to be opened, whereupon attacks from the hostile Queen's Rook will follow, and in the third she is exposed to attack by a Knight at K5. The only way for Black to protect his QKt2 against an attack by White's Queen at QKt3 is to play his Queen to QKt3. He need not fear to allow his Queen's Knight's pawns to be doubled after the exchange of Queens, for the opening of his Queen's Rook's file will give him ample compensation. The pawn at his QKt3 will protect the important squares QB4 and QR4 and will even threaten to advance and attack White's pawn formation.

Thus we arrive at the conclusion that in order to bring out his Queen's Bishop to B4 Black must first protect his Queen's pawn and prepare to play Q—Kt3. The move

P—QB3 achieves both these objects. Now we already see two main lines of defence appearing : either (1) P—QB3 followed by B—B4, giving up the idea of playing P—QB4, or (2) P—QB4, the Queen's pawn being protected by P—K3, in which case the move B—B4 is rendered impossible. A combination of the two moves P—QB4 and B—B4 is impracticable and would open up the game too much ; one can, however, combine the other two ideas, P—QB3 and P—K3, renouncing both P—QB4 and B—B4. This last is the most passive defence, recalling Steinitz's Defence to the Ruy Lopez.

Another question suggests itself : by analogy with the liberating move P—Q4 in the open games, is it not possible in the Queen's Pawn Game for Black to play P—K4 very early ? This move is, of course, very important, since White often plays at his second move Kt—KB3 to prevent it and to command Black's K4. But 2. P—QB4 makes a sort of gambit, comparable with the King's Gambit, and 2. .... P—K4, in reply, a counter-gambit analogous to the Falkbeer (1. P—K4, P—K4 ; 2. P—KB4, P—Q4). It is, however, not difficult to understand that in the Queen's Pawn Game, this counter-gambit will not have the same force, for White's King's position is not weakened as it is by P—KB4 in the King's Gambit.

The advance P—K4 is therefore better as a masked threat like the move P—Q4 in the Ruy Lopez. It is made use of, however, in one variation of the Queen's Gambit Accepted ; if, after 1. P—Q4, P—Q4 ; 2. P—QB4, P×P, White plays 3. P—K3 to regain the pawn sacrificed, Black replies with 3. .... P—K4 and equalises the game with ease. So, in the accepted gambit, White should play 3. Kt—KB3 before thinking of recovering his pawn.

This brings us to another important question : Should the gambit be accepted or declined ?

In the King's Gambit, as we have seen, Black, by playing P—KKt4, can always hold on to the pawn he has gained and if he does not always play this move, it is because of the weakening of the castled position which results from it. In the Queen's Gambit, there is no question of the castled position and it seems quite natural to take the pawn if it can be held.

Unfortunately, White can always regain his pawn, for

Black, in trying to keep it at all costs, only causes his pawn formation to be broken up and create "weaknesses."

Suppose that after 1. P—Q4, P—Q4 ; 2. P—QB4, P×P ; 3. P—K3, Black defends his pawn by 3. .... P—QKt4, then, after 4. P—QR4, 4. .... P—QR3 is inadequate to maintain its defence, because if White plays 5. P×P, Black's Rook's pawn cannot recapture as his Rook is not defended. 4. .... P—QB3 is no more satisfactory because after 5. P×P, P×P ; 6. Q—B3 wins the Queen's Rook. White has yet a further means of attacking the pawn in question by 4. P—QKt3 and, if now 4. .... P×P ; then 5. B×P ch followed by Q×P wins back the pawn.

But we have said that Black can play 3. .... P—K4 and that to prevent it White must lose a tempo by 3. Kt—KB3. Can Black retain the pawn in this case ?   Suppose the game develops as follows : 1. P—Q4, P—Q4 ; 2. P—QB4, P×P ; 3. Kt—KB3, P—QKt4 ; 4. P—K3, P—QR3 ; 5. P—QR4, P—QB3 ; 6. P×P, BP×P ; 7. P—QKt3, B—K3 ; 8. P×P, P×P ; 9. Q—R4 ch, regaining the pawn.

It follows, then, that Black can never keep the pawn gained.   Should he on this account decline the gambit ? He must at all events give up the idea of holding on to the pawn.   But, if he does not take the pawn immediately and plays the defensive move 2. .... P—QB3, he does threaten to take it at some other time and possibly even to retain it, since the move P—QKt4 is already prepared.   However, the idea of this defence is quite different for it actually uses these two moves to attack White's King's Bishop when it recaptures the pawn, and thus to mobilise the whole of the Queen's side without loss of time and with chances of a counter-attack.   Sometimes, too, Black can gain a tempo by accepting the gambit : after White's King's Bishop moves to K2 or Q3, Black plays P×P and forces the Bishop to recapture and lose a tempo in doing so.   Thus, if Black decides to accept the gambit he must only do so with a definite strategical or tactical object.   In general, however, the capture of the pawn is not to be recommended.   You exchange a Queen's pawn for a Queen's Bishop's pawn and almost entirely give up the centre to White who will add to his central Queen's pawn another pawn at K3 or K4.   You will have only the square Q4 at your disposal, and even if one of your pieces is posted there, it will be dislodged very easily by P—K4. This pawn can then advance to K5, owing to the absence of your Queen's pawn, and will drive your Knight from KB3 and threaten the entry of an enemy piece at Q6. From this there arises the possibility of attack on KR2 and a lasting pressure on the centre maintained by the King's Bishop which will be posted at QB4. Such are the disadvantages of accepting the gambit, which one may do, however, if one obtains strategic or tactical compensations as we have pointed out previously.

All these considerations with regard to the accepted gambit bring to light the importance of the move P—QB3. This move allows the sortie of Black's Queen's Bishop and threatens also the capture of White's Queen's Bishop's pawn followed by P—QKt4 and the mobilisation of all Black's Queen's side. Further, it opens a diagonal for the Black Queen. But this is not for the purpose of attacking either White's pawn at QKt2, which is easily defended, or the pawn at Q4 which is not even attacked by a pawn, but rather to pin White's Queen's Knight after it has moved to QB3. Obviously, the attack by the Black Queen (Q—R4) has no force in itself and is just a demonstration, but it initiates a series of moves which will lessen White's pressure on the centre, accelerate the development of Black's pieces and, in preparing for a counter-offensive on the Queen's side, check White's attack.

First of all, the Queen's sortie to R4 is senseless unless White's Queen's Bishop has already been moved out, for the pinning of the Queen's Knight has no point if it can be unpinned by B—Q2. If the Bishop has moved to KKt5, the Black Queen at QR4 threatens it indirectly, for Black's Queen's pawn can always take White's QBP ; further the moving of the Queen unpins the Black Knight at KB3. On the other hand, this unpinning is only permissible if the Knight is defended by another piece, for Black cannot allow the doubling of his King's Bishop's pawn. If the Knight is defended by B—K2, this Bishop will be unable to take part in a counter-offensive on the Queen's side or must lose a tempo in doing so. It is therefore better to defend the Knight with the other Knight by playing QKt—Q2. After Q—R4, the attack can be reinforced by

B—Kt5 followed by Kt—K5. Thus most of Black's pieces are in action and his centre is solid, and it only remains for him to develop his Queen's Bishop. It goes without saying that the whole of this manœuvre must be preceded by the moves P—K3 and P—QB3, and we see that these two moves, which seemingly, can lead only to one of the most passive of defences, may be the start of a full counter-attack on the Queen's side.

After having reviewed the majority of the defences open to Black, it remains for us to specify the different threats at White's disposal. As our explanation has proceeded we have already mentioned some possibilities ; pressure on the centre, an eventual King's side attack, a pressure along the open Queen's Bishop's file, an attack against the weakened Queen's side pawns. White's initiative extends, therefore, perceptibly over the whole board and is summarised in the following facts : (1) White has a pawn at QB4 while Black's is at QB3. (2) His Queen's Knight is at QB3 while Black's is at Q2. (3) White's QB has been developed while Black's is still at QB1. (4) White's King's Bishop is in an active position at Q3 or QB4, while Black's King's Bishop is at K2 defending the pinned Knight. These are small positional advantages comparable to those we have seen in the Ruy Lopez, with the difference that here we are in a full positional game based on this sort of advantage, while in the Ruy Lopez it was practically solely a question of freedom of action for the pieces. That is why it is more dangerous in these openings to rush things, for small advantages are liable to vanish on the slightest inaccuracy. Now is the time to recall the essential rule for the conduct of a game : if one has an advantage in tempo, one should proceed by means of threats so that one's opponent cannot recover the lost time ; if one has an advantage in space, it is, above all, important not to allow one's opponent to break out of his cramped position. This implies not so much threats as constant control of the important squares of his position so that his pieces cannot free themselves. To increase this advantage in space, one must try to cramp the hostile position still more, by making use of what we have learned about strong and weak squares, by placing one's pieces on the best squares, by unobtrusively introducing some future threat to make the

defence more complicated.   Black will seek to free himself
from the hostile pressure by counter-attacks or by exchanges
—for nothing is better in a cramped position than to exchange
passive, badly-placed pieces for the active, well-developed
pieces of the enemy.   However, do not forget that, as a result,
his remaining pieces will have more scope.

We shall now examine some of the methods of attack and
defence in this complicated opening and to illustrate a few
of the tendencies that we have noticed rather than to verify
isolated variations.   Thus, we shall follow, as far as possible,
the various types of defences that we have already considered.

QUEEN'S PAWN GAME

(1. P—Q4, P—Q4 ; 2. KT—KB3)

Let us begin first of all with a passive game on White's
part and suppose that he does not play P—QB4 either at the
second move or at a later stage of the opening.   It is obvious
that if Black replies in an equally passive manner (which
leads to the ordinary variations of the Queen's Gambit) he
will obtain no advantage whatsoever.   His only hope of
securing the initiative rests in playing 2. .... P—QB4, a kind
of gambit a move behind.   But this procedure is not without
risk, and one must fully understand where it is leading
before using it.

COLLE'S SYSTEM

1.	P—Q4	P—Q4
2.	Kt—KB3	P—QB4

2. .... Kt—KB3 or 2. .... P—K3 are good moves but
quieter.

3.   P—B3

A rather more energetic continuation is 3. P—B4, Kt—KB3;
4. BP×P, P×P; 5 Q×P, Q×P; 6. Kt—B3, Q×Q; 7. Kt×Q,
P—QR3, etc.   Black is several moves behind but White's
advantage is not very great.   3. P—QB3 is the basis of Colle's
system in which the main idea is to play P(K3)—K4 as soon
as possible before Black succeeds in playing a similar move.
3. P—B3 defends White's Queen's pawn.   Thus White gives
up all idea of Queen's side operations and decides to attack
the centre and eventually on the King's side.

3.	....	Kt—KB3
4.	P—K3	QKt—Q2
5.	QKt—Q2	P—K3
6.	B—Q3	B—K2
7.	O—O	O—O
8.	P—K4	QP×P
9.	Kt×P	P—QKt3
10.	P×P	P×P
11.	Q—B2	B—Kt2
12.	Kt×Kt ch	Kt×Kt

with a more or less even game.

QUEEN'S GAMBIT

(1. P—Q4, P—Q4 ; 2. P—QB4)

We now pass on to a more active game on White's part, namely, the Queen's Gambit, which has P—QB4 as its second move. Before tackling the normal defences, we shall first take a glance at the immediate counter-gambit 2. .... P—K4.

ALBIN COUNTER-GAMBIT

| 1. | P—Q4 | P—Q4 |
| 2. | P—QB4 | P—K4 |

This counter-gambit can also be played a move later, *i.e.*, 2. .... P—QB3 ; 3. Kt—QB3, P—K4 (Winawer Gambit).

| 3. | QP×P | P—Q5 |
| 4. | Kt—KB3 | |

Beware ! A famous trap. If White plays 4. P—K3 ?, Black wins as follows : 4. .... B—Kt5 ch ; 5. B—Q2, P×P ; 6. B×B, P×P ch ; 7. K—K2, P×Kt (= Kt) ch ; and wins.

QUESTION 23. How would you continue this trap variation?

4.	....	Kt—QB3
5.	QKt—Q2	B—K3
6.	Kt—Kt3	B—Kt5 ch
7.	B—Q2	Q—K2
8.	Q—B2	

or alternatively

| 8. | B×B | Q×B ch |
| 9. | Q—Q2 | Q×P |

10.	R—B1	Q—Q4
11.	R—B5	Q—Q2
12.	QKt×P	

White holds the pawn he has gained.

In general White has nothing to fear from this gambit. His position is not weakened and Black's pressure does not compensate for the pawn lost.

Now let us look at the normal defences.

THE ORTHODOX DEFENCE

(1. P—Q4, P—Q4 ; 2. P—QB4, P—K3 ; 3. KT—QB3, KT—KB3)

As in the Ruy Lopez, Black is quite at liberty to defend passively as his position does not show any weakness. He will hold on to the centre as long as possible and develop his pieces slowly, putting on to White the onus of building up an attack, and himself taking advantage of every exchange to free his own position.

THE ORTHODOX DEFENCE

1.	P—Q4	P—Q4
2.	P—QB4	P—K3
3.	Kt—QB3	Kt—KB3
4.	B—Kt5	B—K2
5.	P—K3	QKt—Q2
6.	Kt—B3	O—O

Consider this position very carefully.

NO. 23.   POSITION AFTER BLACK'S 6TH MOVE

White has developed all his pieces. How should he continue ? If he moves his King's Bishop he will lose a tempo because Black will immediately reply with P×P. If, in order to avoid this loss of a tempo, White exchanges by 7. P×P, P×P, he facilitates the development of Black's Queen's Bishop ; if, instead, he plays 7. P—B5, Black obtains the advantage by playing P—K4 after P—QB3. If White makes a waiting move, e.g., P—QR3, Black can make a symmetrical reply P—QR3. White has no other choice than to move his Queen or Queen's Rook. Now it is Black who has to make an important decision. If White plays 7. R—B1, Black must consolidate the centre by 7. .... P—B3. But after 7. Q—B2, which does not reinforce the attack, Black can play 7. .... P—B4 instead of 7. .... P—B3, and after 8. R—Q1, he can make the move that we have met before, namely, 8. .... Q—R4, threatening the Bishop indirectly. Therefore, remember this carefully : after 7. R—B1, the only possible reply is 7. .... P—B3 ; but after 7. Q—B2, there is a choice between 7. .... P—B3 and 7. .... P—B4.

7.	R—B1	P—B3
8.	B—Q3	P×P
9.	B×P	Kt—Q4
10.	B×B	Q×B
11.	O—O	Kt×Kt
12.	R×Kt	P—K4
13.	P×P	Kt×P
14.	Kt×Kt	Q×Kt

A very much simplified position and approximately even, although White may obtain some sort of attack by P—B4 ; in exchange for this his King's pawn will be weak.

QUESTION 24. Where would you think of retiring the Black Queen after 15. P—B4 ? What continuations can you suggest for White and for Black ?

ACTIVE DEFENCES

We have already pointed out two lines of play in the active defence : firstly, the advance of the Queen's Bishop's pawn to B4, and secondly the sortie of the Queen's Bishop. These we shall examine separately : also a Queen's side counterattack by Black's pieces will be the object of special study.

TARRASCH'S DEFENCE

(1. P—Q4, P—Q4 ; 2. P—QB4, P—K3 ; 3. KT—QB3, P—QB4)

Instead of defending the centre and in particular his Queen's pawn by solid moves as is done in the orthodox or normal defence, Black here decides to oppose his opponent's plans with an attack on the White Queen's pawn. By P—QB4 he gets rid of the backward pawn at QB2 and allows his Queen's Knight to come out at QB3 instead of Q2. In spite of these advantages gained, Black's game does not present any less difficulty, a natural consequence of a counter-offensive in the opening. White has a choice of advantages to exploit. First he can isolate the Queen's pawn and concentrate his whole attack on it, or he may create weaknesses in Black's position which will serve him as strong squares— in fact, all the squares round Black's QP, the defence of which will immobilise all the available forces, are weak. However, it must not be thought that Black's game is already lost : the isolated Queen's pawn may become very strong, and, in the words of Dr. Tarrasch, "He who fears to have an isolated Queen's pawn should give up chess." If this pawn demands the co-operation of several pieces for its defence in the opening, it becomes later on not only an important support for pieces in the centre, but a sort of wedge in the hostile position which it will eventually pierce.

As an illustration of this most important and not less interesting problem of the isolated Queen's pawn, we shall next consider the different results in two positions of this type.

NO 24.   POSITION AFTER WHITE'S 23RD MOVE
(Burn *v.* Znosko-Borovsky, Ostend Tournament, 1906)

The remaining moves were : 23. .... P—Q5 ; 24. P—K4, Kt—K4 ; 25. R—Kt3, Kt(K2)—B3 ; 26. Kt—Q2, Kt×B ; 27 R×Kt, Kt—K4 ; 28. R—KKt3, P—Q6 ; 29. Q—Kt2, R—QB3 ; 30. Kt—B3, Kt×Kt ; 31. Q×Kt, R—B8 ; 32. R(Kt3)—Kt1, R×R ; 33. R×R, Q—Q7 ; 34, R—QKt1, Q—K7 ; 35 Q—Kt2, Q—K6 ; 36. R—Q1, P—Q7 ; 37. P—KR3, Q—K8 ch ; 38. Q—Kt1, Q—K7 ; 39. P—K5, R—Q6, and White resigned.

In this position, the strength of the isolated pawn—which becomes a passed pawn—is clearly shown. This pawn, behind which the Black pieces are massed, forces its way through the hostile pieces ; White cannot even exchange it without allowing Black's pieces to penetrate his lines.

NO. 25. POSITION AFTER WHITE'S 15TH MOVE
(Capablanca *v.* Rubinstein, Berlin Tournament, 1928

The continuation was as follows : 15. .... P—Q5 ; 16. B—Q2, Q—B3 ; 17. R—K4, QR—Q1 ; 18. QR—K1, Q—B3 ; 19. P—Kt3, KR—K1 ; 20. B—R5, R×R ; 21. Q×R, Kt—B1 ; 22. Q×Q, P×Q ; 23. R—K7, R—Q4 ; 24. B×B, P×B ; 25. R—Kt7, Kt—Q2 ; 26. R—B7, R—Q3 ; 27. R—B8 ch, Kt—B1 ; 28. Kt—Q2, P—QB4 ; 29. Kt—B4, R—K3 ; 30. R—Kt8, R—K8 ch ; 31. K—-Kt2, P—KKt4 ; 32. P—QR4, R—QR8 ; 33. Kt×P, and wins.

In this position the pawn does not play such a strong part, not because it is actually weak, but because Black makes a

serious mistake at his 15th move by advancing it too soon
to Q5 on a Black square where it blocks its own pieces and
obliges them to defend it.   In its advance, the pawn should
free its pieces and not confine them to its defence ; it must
then either embed itself in the enemy position, or sacrifice
itself to allow the pieces to penetrate there.   Kept at Q4,
the pawn would have allowed the Black pieces to be deployed
until the right moment when the advance to Q5 would have
yielded the desired result.

Let us now look at some variations of this defence.

1.	P—Q4	P—Q4
2.	P—QB4	P—K3
3.	Kt—QB3	P—QB4
4.	BP×P	

Better than 4. Kt—B3, which would allow Black to obtain
a good game by 4. .... BP×P ; 5. KKt×P, P—K4 ;
6. KKt—Kt5, P—Q5 ; 7. Kt—Q5, Kt—QR3 ; etc.

4.	....	KP×P

The Duisberg Gambit is not recommended, *e.g.*, 4. ....
BP×P ; 5. Q—R4 ch, B—Q2 ; 6. Q×QP, P×P ; 7. Q×QP,
Kt—QB3 ; 8. P—K3, Kt—B3 ; 9. Q—Q1, etc.

5.	Kt—B3	Kt—QB3
6.	P—KKt3	Kt—B3
7.	B—Kt2	

White concentrates all his pieces on the isolated Queen's
pawn (Rubinstein's variation).

7.	....	B—K2
8.	O—O	O—O
9.	P×P	B×P

We may also point out the following gambit of which
Dr. Tarrasch was the great advocate : 9. .... P—Q5 ;
10. Kt—QR4, B—B4, etc.

10.	Kt—QR4	B—K2
11.	B—K3	

observing the squares Q4 and QB5.

11.	....	Kt—K5
12.	Kt—Q4	Kt×Kt

Black has a free game but White also has many resources.

QUESTION 25.   How should the game be continued if
White plays B—Kt5 at either the 9th or 10th move ?

CZECH DEFENCE

(1. P—Q4, P—Q4 ; 2. P—QB4, P—QB3)

This defence, as active as the preceding one, has for its objects the development of the Queen's Bishop at B4 and the mobilisation of the Queen's side by P×P and P—QKt4, sometimes followed by P—QB4 or P—Kt5 ; this last mobilisation can dispense with the development of the Queen's Bishop and slightly resembles the counter-attack in the Ruy Lopez by P—QR3, P—QKt4, P—QB4.

The move P—QB3 is the starting-point of these two manœuvres, and White must not under-estimate either these or, more particularly, the taking of the gambit pawn, for as we have already seen, after P×P Black can defend his pawn by P—QKt4. White has now the choice between two tactical plans. He may either prevent the above-mentioned mobilisation, by doing which he will allow the immediate sortie of Black's Queen's Bishop to B4, or he may allow Black to advance his pawns on the Queen's side, speculating upon their becoming weak. We shall examine the trend of these two ideas.

(a) DR. KRAUSE'S VARIATION

1.	P—Q4	P—Q4
2.	P—QB4	P—QB3
3.	Kt—KB3	

We are already aware of the importance of this move : once P×P is threatened, Kt—KB3 must be played to prevent P—K4 next move.

3.	....	Kt—B3
4.	Kt—B3	

The Knight is better posted at QB3 than at Q2. However, if the Queen's Bishop's pawn has previously been taken, the Knight can then be developed at Q2 so as to recapture the pawn at QB4 and afterwards to occupy K5. But this manœuvre is not always possible.

4.	....	P×P
5.	P—QR4	

To prevent 5. .... P—QKt4.

5.	....	B—B4
6.	Kt—K5	QKt—Q2

QUESTION 26.   What continuation has Black to fear if he plays 5. .... P—K3 ? How would you reply if, in the main variation, Black played 6. .... P—K3 ?

7.	Kt×P (B4)	Q—B2
8.	P—KKt3	P—K4

Black has attained his strategical objective : it is not surprising that his position is somewhat open.

9.	P×P	Kt×P
10.	B—B4	KKt—Q2
11.	B—Kt2	B—K3
12.	Kt×Kt	Kt×Kt
13.	O—O	B—K2

with a lively game.

(b) ALEKHINE'S VARIATION

1.	P—Q4	P—Q4
2.	P—QB4	P—QB3
3.	Kt—KB3	Kt—B3
4.	Kt—B3	P×P
5.	P—K3	P—QKt4
6.	P—QR4	P—Kt5
7.	Kt—R2	

7. Kt—QKt1 is playable, e.g., 7. Kt—QKt1, B—R3 ; 8. KKt—Q2, Q—Q4 ; 9. Q—B2, P—K3 ; 10. Kt×P, B—K2 ; 11. QKt—Q2, etc.

7.	....	P—K3
8.	B×P	QKt—Q2

Black must do everything possible to play P—QB4 quickly and must never lose sight of White's threatened advance P—K4 and P—K5.

9.	O—O	B—Kt2
10.	Q—K2	P—B4
11.	R—Q1	Q—Kt3

Giving up the idea of playing his Queen's Bishop to B4, Black has developed it at Kt2 and has mobilised the whole of his Queen's side. The game is full of possibilities for both players.

QUEEN'S SIDE COUNTER-ATTACK
(6. .... Q—R4 AND 7. .... B—KT5)

A player who, as Black, starts a Queen's side counter-attack in the Queen's Gambit must not delude himself about the outcome of his enterprise. This demonstration, without going so far as to demolish White's position, at least allows Black to bring out his pieces with threats and thus without loss of time. He will thus complete his development and will be able to resume a normal game.

As we have indicated, this counter-attack is based on a slight weakness in White's position due to the moving of his Queen's Bishop and the advance of the Queen's Bishop's pawn to B4. What we have said of the danger to Black of playing B—KB4 is still more true of the sortie of White's Queen's Bishop, especially after P—QB4. Further White must be on his guard not to lose this pawn, and then, having repulsed the first attack, he will recapture the initiative and Black will sometimes be compelled to beat a retreat.

Let us repeat the conditions essential to Black's counter-attack : defence of his Knight at KB3 by a Knight at Q2, the holding back of his King's Bishop at B1 until the moment it joins in the attack, and the preliminary moves P—K3 and P—QB3. The first few moves in this defence are therefore made in the following order : 1. P—Q4, P—Q4 ; 2. P—QB4, P—K3 ; 3. Kt—QB3, Kt—KB3 ; 4. B—Kt5, QKt—Q2 ; 5. P—K3, P—B3 ; 6. Kt—B3.

We thus observe the first difference between this and the normal defence : at the 4th move Black here plays QKt—Q2 instead of B—K2. As a matter of fact, there is very little to choose between these two moves, and the order of playing them can be reversed : by 6. .... B—K2 Black can transpose into the variation with which we are already familiar. But if he wishes to carry out this counter-attack, the Cambridge Springs Defence, he must leave his Bishop at KB1 in order to develop it at Kt5 at the appropriate moment.

Beware ! A pretty trap.

The move 4. .... QKt—Q2, so inoffensive in appearance, is, nevertheless, of great interest, for it hides a subtle trap. The pinned Knight at B3 no longer defends Black's Queen's pawn, and by playing 4. .... QKt—Q2 Black does not unpin it, leaving the pawn, therefore, without defence. Why, then, should not White take it ? After 5. P×P, P×P ; 6. Kt×P, the Black Knight cannot recapture for it is pinned ! But that is precisely the trap, for Black replies with 6. .... Kt×Kt, sacrificing his Queen, and after 7. B×Q, B—Kt5 ch ;

8. Q—Q2, B×Q ch he wins back his Queen and remains a piece to the good.

Remember this little trap but note that it is not possible when the White King has a flight square or when White's King's Knight is at B3 and is thus able to interpose at Q2.

CAMBRIDGE SPRINGS DEFENCE

1.	P—Q4	P—Q4
2.	P—QB4	P—K3
3.	Kt—QB3	Kt—KB3
4.	B—Kt5	QKt—Q2
5.	P—K3	P—B3
6.	Kt—B3	Q—R4

The starting-point of this defence. The Queen indirectly threatens the Bishop at KKt5 and pins the Knight, which will be further attacked by B—Kt5 and Kt—K5.

7.   Kt—Q2

The exchange of the Bishop for the Knight is not recommendable, e.g., 7. B×Kt, Kt×B ; 8. B—Q3, B—Kt5 ; 9. Q—Kt3, P×P ; 10. B×BP, O—O ; etc. It is better to play 7. P×P, Kt×P ; 8. Q—Q2, B—Kt5 ; 9. R—B1, P—KR3 ; 10. B—R4, O—O ; 11. B—Q3, P—K4 ; etc. The text move, while unpinning the Knight, also protects White's K4.

7.	....	B—Kt5
8.	Q—B2	O—O
9.	B—K2	

White can play instead 9. B—R4 or 9. B×Kt.

QUESTION 27. In this variation, why does White play his Bishop to K2 and not to Q3, and why would this latter move be a bad one ?

| 9. | .... | P—K4 |

This move, freeing the Queen's Bishop, plays an important part in this defence. Sometimes, as in the first variation in the note following White's 7th move, the Bishop is developed at QKt2 or QR3, after P—QKt3.

10.	QP×P	Kt—K5
11.	KKt×Kt	P×Kt
12.	O—O	B×Kt
13.	P×B	

Possibly White would do better to play for an end-game by 13. Q×B.

| 13. | .... | Kt×P |

14.	Q×P	Kt—Kt3
15.	B—B4	Kt×B
16.	Q×Kt	Q×BP

Black has surmounted the difficulties of the opening. In conclusion, it should be pointed out that White can avoid the Cambridge Springs Defence by playing 6. P—QR3 instead of 6. Kt—B3.

DUTCH DEFENCE

(1. P—Q4, P—KB4)

We have seen that in both the Queen's Pawn Game and Queen's Gambit the attack on Black's Queen's pawn by P—QB4 and later by P(K3)—K4 confronts him with a difficult problem. He has to choose between an isolated Queen's pawn, to exchange that pawn and abandon the centre, or to allow the advance of White's King's pawn to K5. Can he not escape all these difficulties by eliminating the move 1. .... P—Q4 and replacing it by 1. .... P—KB4 ? White's second move P—QB4 would thus lose its effect and the advance of White's King's pawn to K4 would enable Black to open the King's Bishop's file for attacking purposes. It is not a gambit, however, for Black does not give up a pawn : it does not weaken the castled position, as does the same move by White in the King's Gambit, because P—K3 will protect him against the threat of B—QB4. Whether White plays P—K4 early or late, Black can exchange or not, as he likes. His Queen's side is safe and offers no point for attack, while his centre, although backward, is solid. However, he is "exposed" in another sense of the word. By making the move 1. .... P—KB4, he commits himself to an attack on the King's side, and it is always bad to show one's hand too soon. Furthermore, this attack is difficult to carry out because of the lack of openings for his Bishops.

Of course, if he develops his Queen's Bishop at Q2, it cannot take part in the attack ; if he develops it at Kt2 his opponent will oppose it with his King's Bishop and bring about an exchange, which will weaken Black's attack. As for Black's King's Bishop, it is difficult to see how this can help. It may very well prejudice development if it stays at K2, while if it is placed at Q3, in front of the Queen's pawn,

it hinders the operations of the other pieces. The best
solution would be to exchange it for White's Queen's
Bishop by playing B—Kt5 ch, and it is for this reason that
White sometimes avoids playing P—QB4 before castling.
Black's attack, therefore, includes only the Queen (via K1
and R4), the Knight (moving to KKt5), and the King's
Bishop's pawn which either advances to B5 or opens the
King's Bishop's file for the Rook, according to circumstances.

What should be White's tactics in this opening ? He must
for the time being give up his operations on the Queen's
side and by a well-thought-out defence on the King's side
compel his opponent to engage as many pieces as possible
in the attack which he will gradually master. Above all, he
must concentrate on the centre by free play of his pieces and
by controlling all the important squares. Then, if Black does
not follow up his attack, White will get an advantage simply
by positional play, and if his attack is repulsed, his downfall
will be only the more rapid.

In the Dutch Defence, we notice the appearance, for the
first time, of the idea of a backward centre, for Black builds
up a central pawn position in retreat and prepares a counter-
attack on White's King's side. We shall see all these ideas
brought out in the two groups of openings that we are now
going to examine. We shall study the importance of them
more thoroughly later on ; for the moment we take note of
them in passing.

We give now the main lines of play of the Dutch Defence.

(a)

1.	P—Q4	P—K3
2.	P—QB4	P—KB4
3.	P—KKt3	Kt—KB3
4.	B—Kt2	B—Kt5 ch
5.	Kt—Q2	Kt—K5
6.	P—QR3	Kt × Kt
7.	B × Kt	B × B ch
8.	Q × B	O—O
9.	Kt—R3	

Notice that Black does not play P—KB4 until the second
move. It can also be played as first move, but then Black
runs the risk of White sacrificing his King's pawn (Blackmar
Gambit) and refuting this somewhat anti-positional move.

(b)

1.	P—Q4	P—KB4
2.	P—K4	P×P
3.	Kt—QB3	Kt—KB3
4.	B—KKt5	

Alternatively 4. P—B3, P—Q4 ; 5. B—KKt5.

4.	. . . .	P—B3
5.	P—B3	P×P
6.	Kt×P	Q—Kt3
7.	Q—Q2	P—Q3
8.	O—O—O	

White has a very well-developed game and great attacking chances : after all, it is all that Black deserves.

THIRD GROUP

HALF-OPEN GAMES

(1. P—K4, OTHER REPLIES THAN P—K4)

On the whole, Black should not be dissatisfied with what the modern theory of openings offers him. Up to the present we have been able to show that in both the open and close openings certain continuations assure him equality and sometimes even give him the better game. In variations where the advantage of the move has a more lasting effect, his position is never desperate—far from it.

His happiness would be complete if only he could choose the opening. But after 1. P—K4, P—K4, or 1. P—Q4, P—Q4, it rests with White to decide the course of the game and Black has nothing better to do than to follow either with an energetic defence or a counter-attack. But White gives a very definite turn to the game so that even in the quietest variations, he retains the advantage of the move. Black has to struggle, laboriously at times, to neutralise this advantage and sees that he is powerless against symmetry of position in its wider sense.

Thinking thus, Black may well look for some other system of opening which will give to the game a direction of his own choosing and so liberate him from the yoke White imposes on him. Immediate asymmetry of position will remove the importance of the move.

Theoretically, we have seen that White should always increase this initial advantage and should not allow Black to equalise, but Black may have other ideas and may not be content with something approaching equality; he may even in the early stages hope to win. The character of the half-open games lends itself very well to such ideas, even though the fear of White's attacks may have given rise to them.

Now let us try to give the chief characteristics of the half-open games. Black attempts to meet White's King-centre with another type of centre, usually a Queen-centre. Thus the game develops into a struggle between these two centres and the position is totally unsymmetrical and quite unlike those we have seen in previous openings in which two King-centres or two Queen-centres were opposed, White's being always the active and Black's the passive one. Here both centres may be active and thus the advantage of the move is diminished.

Here are two typical positions taken at random. No. 26 shows an open game with two King-centres, while No. 27 shows a half-open game with White's King-centre opposed by Black's Queen-centre.

NO. 26

NO. 27

Instead of struggling against a King-centre, Black fights the battle round his Queen-centre, where he can be more active. A glance at the two diagrams will show the profound difference between the two types of games. In the half-open games, White is naturally led to attack on the King's side, while Black operates on the Queen's side. It is just as if Black is effecting an enveloping movement, a manœuvre well known in military strategy.

Having first move sometimes becomes even a disadvantage. White commits himself by the move 1. P—K4 and the advanced pawn becomes a target for Black's attacks. Thus the general line of play is obvious. Black must attack the White pawns by his own to break up the centre or, at all events, to weaken it by depriving it of the supporting pawns. Further, as Black establishes a Queen-centre composed of three pawns (the Queen's Knight must never be played in front of the Queen's Bishop's pawn) he will always be more solid in the centre than White.

This solidity is enhanced by the following consideration. White, seeing that the advantage of the move is leaving him, courageously advances his King's and Queen's pawns two squares so as not to yield ground. Black, on the other hand, remains on the defensive on the King's side by forming a backward centre and his pawns are therefore out of White's reach. The two White pawns form an advanced centre which attacks nothing, while lack of preparation and precautions makes this advanced centre weak, for White's King's pawn may suddenly become a weakness and demand immediate and constant defence. To the prospect of a battle between a King-centre and a Queen-centre is added that of a struggle between an advanced and a backward centre.

A third aspect of this battle for the centre must be stressed. Up to the present we have referred to the principles of rapid development, of the necessity of hindering hostile development (which is equivalent to a gain of time). We have said nothing about gain of space, i.e., territorial gain.

As a general rule these two gains go together, for in hindering hostile development we necessarily occupy more of the board. Solid openings like the Ruy Lopez and Queen's Gambit have accustomed us to this outlook. It does not necessarily follow, however, since frequently one of the adversaries may gain time while the other gains space. Of course one would desire to have the advantage in all three elements—force, space and time—but this is almost impossible. The diversity of chess is such that the exact appreciation of each position demands the greatest finesse. It is sometimes difficult to decide whether the gain in one element is equal, inferior, or superior to that in another. In the openings—leaving out gain or loss of material in consequence of a gambit or a mistake—space and time have by no means the same value. We gain time by getting ahead of our opponent in development, and that is of prime importance. We occupy more space by advancing our pawns and that is sometimes dangerous. It is a good plan to harass the enemy and to drive him back by gaining ground and so make the movement of his pieces more difficult, but it is precisely here that the solidity of his position justifies itself; it is like a spring whose force increases as it is compressed.

Suddenly, because the pawns which have been used to gain space cannot retire, they become a weakness, and this fortress which seemed to give us an incontestable advantage, crumbles like a house of cards. Advantage in space is more apparent than one in time, but appearances are often deceptive. In this, the inner meaning of a position has some bearing on its outer form. It is preferable to give up the idea of occupying advanced posts unless we can maintain or defend them. Every advanced post is, by reason of its proximity to the enemy position, very exposed to attack, the danger of which is less when it is occupied by pieces, for they can retire; but with pawns this danger may become catastrophic.

The backward centre is like an ambush. It sacrifices space, just as a gambit sacrifices a pawn, but the opponent can accept neither sacrifice without circumspection. One must not launch a pawn attack on a backward centre without preparation.

These ideas which have not been of use to us up to the present, throw light upon the openings left for us to study, namely, those based on symmetrical formations and those following a different line of play for both White and Black. It is for such reasons that certain theoreticians are led to say that 1. P—K4 may be considered a decisive mistake. This pawn, already weak because it is undefended, becomes weaker still by advancing. Black, reserving to himself the right of forming a backward centre, can attack it at his leisure, or, by playing P—Q4, can even make a counter-attack with his strong Queen's pawn.

Thus we may observe the stages through which the half-open game has passed. First, an ordinary defence to an open game, then an asymmetric attempt to challenge the advantage of the move, and finally the evolution of a new mode of attack against the "weak" White formation. So these openings develop on quite modern lines, for they introduce a struggle between time (the dynamic element) and space (the static element).

A position taken from one of these openings will soon show the comparative values of gains in time and in space.

NO. 28.   POSITION AFTER BLACK'S 6TH MOVE

Count the number of moves made by White and by Black and note also the squares occupied by each side. White has certainly gained possession of the important squares Q4 and K5, but has paid for this by loss of time.

In the half-open games, there is, then, a combination of three plans : (1) Queen-centre v. King-centre ; (2) Backward centre v. Advanced centre ; (3) Attack on White's King's pawn. These ideas are more or less interwoven in each one of these openings, *e. g.*, the second and third appear together in Alekhine's Defence. However, in all these defences, Black's operations plainly start on the Queen's side.

So in order to sub-divide these openings according to their most marked characteristic, we shall base our grouping on the essential idea and classify them in the following manner :

(1) Formation of a Queen-centre by Black. (a) French Defence, (b) Caro-Kann Defence, (c) Sicilian Defence.

(2) Attack on White's King's pawn. (a) Centre Counter, (b) Alekhine's Defence.

What tactics should White adopt in these openings ? First of all, he must never give way to his opponent. The goal Black is aiming at has not yet been reached, and it still rests with him to justify what is only an intention. Let White, on the contrary, show the correctness of his own point of view, and prove that Black is wrong. Moltke once said, "He is beaten who has defeat at heart," and Marshal Foch has paraphrased this dictum in the words, "He is beaten who first feels himself beaten." So White must not forget that his operations on the King's side carry threats more dangerous than his opponent's demonstrations on the Queen's side, for in the former case mate may ensue, while in the latter there can result only an advantage in position or material. White can even accept the challenge on the Queen's side because he is not weakened there. But he must exercise discretion, and must not advance pawns without taking precautions.

FRENCH DEFENCE

When White's pawns are at K4 and Q4 and Black's are at K4 and Q3 we have the usual formation of the open game, but if instead Black's pawns are at K3 and Q4 we have the formation of the French Defence.

The difference may seem insignificant but nevertheless it gives rise to a quite different strategical plan and a system of development, whose effects are immediately felt. In the first formation Black's pawns are passive, while in the second they are active, since White's King's pawn is undefended. If White exchanges pawns a symmetrical position is reached, which means that he has not increased the advantage of the

move. He retains it, of course, but the first three moves
have left the situation unchanged.

To avoid such a result, White may choose to defend his
pawn or to advance it to K5 and so remove it from Black's
attack. At K5, the White pawn may embarrass Black
because it commands the important squares Q6 and KB6.
There is even a possibility of a King's side attack which
Black can best counter by an advance on the Queen's side,
leading to a very active game for both sides. We have
already discussed at length in the preamble of the dangers
attending White's advance of the pawn from K4 to K5.
Black can attack both this pawn and the pawn at Q4 by
P—QB4 and P—KB3. To maintain his centre White must
bring other pawns to its support by playing P—QB3 and
P—KB4.

White has the alternative of exchanging one or both of
his centre pawns (QP×P followed by KP×P), giving up
the centre. The Black pawns at K3 and Q4 on the open
King's and Queen's files will no longer be supported by
other pawns, and at the same time the squares Q4 and K5
cannot now be attacked by Black pawns. The result is that
White can occupy these central squares with pieces to hold
back the Black pawns at K3 and Q4 and to attack them.

If, in spite of all threats, Black succeeds in keeping his
pawns, he will have a formidable weapon for the end-game,
and even before that if he is able to advance them. The
move P—K4, more than any other, seems to be the one
which will decide the issue of the game.

If White protects his King's pawn instead of moving it to
K5, Black multiplies his attacks against White's central
pawns in order to force P—K5. Then the game follows,
more or less, the line of play just described with the difference
that White can choose the best time to make this move,
while Black's pieces, directed on White's K4, will be badly
placed when the pawn reaches K5.

To avoid this less advantageous line of play, Black can
put an end to all ideas of this advance by simply playing
QP×P. The game becomes considerably simplified and
Black must play P—QB4 in order to neutralise White's
pawn at Q4. If White defends it by P—QB3, he will
have an isolated Queen's pawn after Black exchanges pawns

On the other hand, the removal of White's King's pawn will permit Black to obtain command of the long diagonal from his QR1 to KR8 by posting a Bishop at QKt2, foreshadowing an attack against the castled position.

As a general rule, the move P—QB4 by Black plays a very important part in this opening and it must never be prevented by Kt—QB3.

Black must always be on his guard that his Q3, weakened by the move P—QB4, is not occupied by a White piece. The manœuvre Kt(QB3)—Kt5—Q6 by his opponent is to be feared and to parry it he must sometimes play P—QR3 before P—QB4, either to prevent the White Knight from reaching QKt5 or to dislodge it from this square. These remarks presuppose that Black's King's Bishop has been exchanged or has been moved off the diagonal KB1 to QR6 ; otherwise Black's Q3 is sufficiently guarded.

Many amateurs are tempted to block the position after P—QB4 by playing P—QB5. This is a strategical error ; this advance certainly has the advantage of commanding White's Q3, a square which it is essential for White's King's Bishop to occupy for an attack on Black's castled position, but it has the very great drawback that it postpones for a long time any action on the Queen's side. As White will then have no anxiety on this wing or in the centre, he can carry out decisive operations on the King's side at his leisure. Summing up, we find that the move P—QB5 is only justifiable on the rare occasions when it can be followed up by an effective attack on White's pawn at QB3 by P—QKt4 and P—QKt5 ; but this is usually too slow a process.

Having thus sketched out the lines of play characterising this opening, we shall group the various defences as follows :

(1) Exchange of centre pawns either by White or Black.

(2) Advance of White's King's pawn to K5 on the 3rd or 4th move.

(3) The delayed advance P—K5, which gives rise to two systems of defence, (a) Active Defence, (b) Passive o Classical Defence.

(1) EXCHANGE OF THE CENTRAL PAWNS

1.	P—K4	P—K3
2.	P—Q4	P—Q4
3.	Kt—QB3	

We shall not waste time by studying the variations resulting from the exchange of pawns by 3. P×P, P×P, for they present no difficulty at all.

3.	....	Kt—KB3

The exchange of pawns can be made at this point, and practically the same variations occur.

4.	B—Kt5	P×P
5.	Kt×P	

After 5. B×Kt, Black must play P×B and not Q×B because of 6. Kt×P, Q—Q1 with loss of time.

5.	....	B—K2

Black can play instead 5. .... QKt—Q2.

6.	B×Kt	P×B

The quiet move 6. .... B×B offers less chances than the text-move.

7.	Kt—KB3	P—Kt3
8.	B—Kt5 ch	P—B3
9.	B—Q3	B—Kt2

The White Knight must not be dislodged immediately from K4 by P—KB4; this advance, which may weaken Black's position by allowing the threatening move P—Q5, should be made at a more opportune moment.

The position is full of possibilities for both sides. Black's Bishops will have a great deal to do in order to maintain equilibrium, on account of his doubled pawns and of the freedom of action of White's pieces.

(2) THE PAWN ADVANCE (P—K5)

1.	P—K4	P—K3
2.	P—Q4	P—Q4
3.	Kt—QB3	

The immediate advance of White's King's pawn to K5 is not to be recommended as it exposes White to the same attacks (by the moves P—QB4 and P—KB3) as before, and moreover allows the hostile Knight to reach the very important square KB4, via KR3.

3.	....	Kt—KB3
4.	P—K5	KKt—Q2
5.	QKt—K2	

The Gledhill Attack, 5. Q—Kt4, is interesting but Black can defend himself adequately, e.g., 5. .... P—QB4;

6. Kt—Kt5, P×P ; 7. Kt—KB3, Kt—QB3 ; 8. Kt—Q6 ch, B×Kt ; 9. Q×KtP, B×P ; 10. Kt×B, Q—B3 ; etc. (Bogoljubov *v.* Réti, Mährisch-Ostrau Tournament, 1923).

5.	....	P—QB4
6.	P—QB3	Kt—QB3
7.	P—KB4	Q—Kt3
8.	Kt—B3	P—B3

A typical position in the French Defence where the inferiority of White's premature advance, P—K5, is clearly seen, for he has not yet made any definite move on the King's side, and his centre pawns are in danger.

(3) ACTIVE DEFENCE (MCCUTCHEON)

1.	P—K4	P—K3
2.	P—Q4	P—Q4
3.	Kt—QB3	Kt—KB3

Black can instead play 3. .... B—Kt5, but it brings him no advantage, *e.g.*, 3. .... B—Kt5 ; 4. P—K5, P—QB4 ; 5. B—Q2, Kt—QB3 ; 6. P—QR3.

4.	B—Kt5	B—Kt5

Black goes on with his attack on the King's pawn.

5.	P—K5	

An alternative here is 5. P×P, Q×P ; 6. B×Kt, P×B ; 7. Q—Q2, Q—QR4 ; 8. KKt—K2, Kt—Q2, etc. (Capablanca *v.* Bogoljubow, New York Tournament, 1924).

5.	....	P—KR3
6.	B—Q2	

The continuation 6. P×Kt, P×B ; 7. P×P, R—Kt1 ; 8. P—KR4, P×P ; 9. Q—R5, Q—B3 leads to nothing for White.

QUESTION 28. How should the game proceed if the Bishop retreats to another square, *e.g.*, R4 ?

6.	....	B×Kt
7.	P×B	Kt—K5
8.	Q—Kt4	P—KKt3

The move 8. .... K—B1 is not so good, *e.g.*, 8. .... K—B1 ; 9. P—KR4, P—QB4 ; 10. R—R3, Kt—QB3 ; 11. B—Q3, Kt×B ; 12. K×Kt, with rather a strong attack.

9.	B—Q3	Kt×B
10.	K×Kt	P—QB4

The end-game resulting from the exchange of Queens

would be to White's advantage, *e. g.*, 10. .... Q—Kt4 ch ;
11. Q×Q,   P×Q ;   12.   P—KB4,   P×P ;   13.   R—KB1, etc.

11.	P—KR4	Kt—B3
12.	R—R3	P×P
13.	P×P	B—Q2

A position which is far from being lifeless.

(4)   PASSIVE OR CLASSICAL DEFENCE

1.	P—K4	P—K3
2.	P—Q4	P—Q4
3.	Kt—QB3	Kt—KB3
4.	B—Kt5	B—K2
5.	P—K5	

The continuation 5. B×Kt, B×B ; 6. P—K5, B—K2 is
very bad from a theoretical point of view, for White gives
up his valuable Bishop for a Knight and leaves his opponent
with two Bishops.

5.	....	KKt—Q2
6.	P—KR4	

The Alekhine-Chatard Variation.   6. B × B, Q × B; 7. Q—Q2,
O—O ; 8. P—B4 may well be played.

QUESTION 29.   How would you continue this variation if
White played 7. Kt—Kt5 ?

6.	....	P—KR3

The gambit must not be accepted, for 6. .... B×B ;
7. P×B, Q×P ; 8. Kt—R3, Q—K2 ; 9. Kt—B4 gives White
a strong attack.   By playing 6. .... P—KB3 Black may
induce White to sacrifice his Bishop by playing 7. B—Q3,
but as this sacrifice leads to a very strong attack, Black would
be well advised to avoid this variation.

7.	B—K3	

After 7. B×B, Q×B we return to the variation mentioned
in the note to White's 6th move—with the moves P—KR4
and P—KR3 added.

7.	....	P—QB4
8.	Q—Kt4	B—B1

The value of White's 6th move is now obvious, for he
can immediately reinforce his attack by playing R—R3.

9.	P—B4	P×P
10.	B×P	Kt—QB3
11.	Kt—B3	Q—R4
12.	R—R3	P—R4

A difficult position for both sides.

CARO-KANN DEFENCE
(1. P—K4, P—QB3)

The Caro-Kann Defence is very much more passive than the French Defence. Black gives up all idea of attacking the Queen's pawn by P—QB4, a move so important in the French Defence. On the contrary P—QB3 serves only to maintain a pawn at Q4 by allowing him to recapture with a pawn in case of exchange, and thus to keep two pawns in the centre. But if, after exchanging, White continues his attack on the Queen's pawn by P—QB4, Black will find himself compelled to play P—K3 and shut in his Queen's Bishop. We are already aware of the inconveniences of this move which gives White a very much freer game.

But it is quite unnecessary for White to exchange pawns ; he can maintain his centre, confident that he has nothing to fear from Black's attack. It is clear that after a move like 3. Kt—QB3, defending White's King's pawn, Black threatens no good reply. If he plays Kt—KB3 he will lose a tempo since White will play P—K5. His Queen's Knight has no good square, neither has his Queen's Bishop. Further, Black is himself forced to make the exchange of pawns, and the move P—QB3 loses its significance, for its whole object was to recapture with a pawn at Q4, so that Black would not have to give up the centre by taking back with the Queen or another piece.

The passive and temporary nature of the move P—QB3 is more evident from the fact that Black will have to lose a tempo in order to attack White's Queen's pawn by P—QB4, and that after the exchange, he will have no pawns at all on his fourth rank.

However, as a passive defence pure and simple, this opening is quite playable, and White would be making a great mistake in thinking that it is merely a question of an energetic onslaught to break down Black's resistance. The latter's position shows no weaknesses whatever and can in consequence withstand a strong attack.

(a) EXCHANGE OF PAWNS BY WHITE

1.	P—K4	P—QB3
2.	P—Q4	P—Q4
3.	P×P	P×P

4.   P—QB4   Kt—KB3
5.   Kt—QB3   Kt—B3
6.   B—Kt5   P×P

Black ought to give up the idea of developing his Queen's Bishop and play the safer move 6. .... P—K3, with the continuation 7. Kt—B3 (perhaps it is better to play 7. P×P first), P×P ; 8. B×P, B—K2 ; 9. O—O, O—O, with an even game (Botvinnik *v.* Euwe, Hastings Tournament, 1934).

QUESTION 30.   How should this variation be continued after 6. Kt—B3, B—Kt5 ; 7. P×P, KKt×P ; 8. B—QKt5 ?

7.   P—Q5   Kt—K4
8.   Q—Q4   Kt—Q6 ch
9.   B×Kt   P×B
10. Kt—B3

with a strong attack in return for the pawn.

(b)   EXCHANGE OF PAWNS BY BLACK

1.   P—K4   P—QB3
2.   P—Q4   P—Q4
3.   Kt—QB3   P×P
4.   Kt×P

To the gambit move 4. P—KB3, Black has a good reply in 4. .... P—K4, or even better in 4. .... P—K6 with an excellent game.

4.   ....   Kt—KB3

Black can well play 4. .... B—B4 with the continuation 5. Kt—Kt3, B—Kt3 ; 6. Kt—B3, but he must continue with 6. .... Kt—Q2, to stop the White Knight from fixing itself at K5 and attacking the Bishop.

QUESTION 31.   How should White continue after 4. .... B—B4 ; 5. Kt—Kt3, B—Kt3 ; 6. P—KR4, P—KR3 ?

5.   Kt—Kt3

A quieter variation is 5. Kt×Kt ch, KP×Kt ; 6. P—QB3, B—Q3 ; 7. B—Q3, O—O ; 8. Kt—K2, etc.

5.   ....   P—K4

The move 5. .... P—K3 would be wiser.

6.   Kt—B3

Obviously, if 6. P×P, then 6. .... Q×Q ch ; 7. K×Q, Kt—Kt5, etc.

6.	....	P×P
7.	Kt×P	B—QB4

Here 7. .... B—K2 would be wiser.

| 8. | Q—K2 ch | B—K2 |

If 7. .... Q—K2 then 8. Q×Q ch, B×Q ; 9. Kt—B5, and Black is in difficulties.

9.	B—K3	O—O
10.	O—O—O	Q—R4

An interesting position.

SICILIAN DEFENCE

The Sicilian Defence reminds us of the Dutch Defence, the reply to the advance of the King's pawn in the former resembles the reply to the advance of the Queen's pawn in the latter. But the comparison is all in favour of the Sicilian Defence because the advance of the Queen's Bishop's pawn is entirely free from the dangers attending the advance of the King's Bishop's pawn. Further, the object of this defence is far from being so limited as that of the Dutch Defence, for while the latter is confined to an attack on White's castled position, the former comprises a pressure on the Queen's side, a game in the centre and even a possibility of a King's side attack. The comparison is thus in favour of the Sicilian Defence, which like the Dutch Defence, is allied to the ultra-modern openings rather than to the open, close or half-open games.

Of course, in this defence, Black renounces the idea of building up an active centre. He is content with a backward centre formed of pawns on the third rank, and only advances them much later at an opportune moment. He does nothing to prevent White from occupying the central squares—not only those on the fourth rank—but even invites White to advance his pawns to the fifth rank. It is then that the pawns become weak and White's position cracks. Suddenly all the lines are opened for Black's pieces to enter and attack the King. The ideas that we have developed earlier on the value of gain of time and space are applicable here, but we must wait until we come to the ultra-modern openings, starting with Alekhine's Defence, before we obtain full knowledge of this subject.

Black's first idea in the Sicilian Defence is to prevent White creating a centre with pawns at K4 and Q4. By playing 1. .... P—QB4, Black threatens to take the Queen's pawn as soon as it reaches Q4. By this exchange of pawns, Black keeps his two centre pawns while White remains with his King's pawn alone, and this has only one pawn— the King's Bishop's—to support it. At the same time, Black opens his Queen's Bishop's file for a future attack on White's Queen's Bishop's pawn and confronts White with the same problem that we have already had occasion to note in the Queen's Gambit.

It will be recalled that, in the Queen's Gambit, Black should never play his Queen's Knight in front of his Queen's Bishop's pawn. Here, too, White should avoid playing Kt—QB3 before P—QB4 for the same reasons. This last move, as a matter of fact, will neutralise most of Black's threats.

Unfortunately, White often finds himself forced to play Kt—QB3 before P—QB4, and difficulties arise. The weakness of his King's pawn soon forces him to make that natural defensive move. Black has only to combine P—QB4 with an attack on the King's pawn to achieve the desired result, that of making White play his Queen's Knight in front of his Queen's Bishop's pawn.

Black's line of play is clearly defined : a rapid development on the Queen's side with pressure on the Queen's Bishop's file and eventually an attack on that wing. His Queen's Bishop at QKt2 will control the centre and may also threaten the King's side. He develops his pieces slowly and has a backward centre in the expectation of being able to advance it later on.

White's game, too, is an active one. He can obviously attack on the King's side, or pierce the centre and take up the challenge on the Queen's side, where he has a pawn superiority of three to two. However, he must be very careful in preparing an attack on the King's side and King-centre. Nevertheless, never forget that he has the advantage in time and space and that in spite of the dangers of a precipitate advance, he has the right to expect it to succeed if it is carefully prepared. Black, in fact, has reduced his mobility by forming his backward centre. He finds

some difficulty in usefully developing his King's Bishop, for,
if he advances his King's pawn, the Bishop must guard his
Q3 and remain inactive for some time. He can develop it
more actively at KKt2, after playing P—KKt3, but this
formation is not without danger, since White is preparing
for an attack on the castled position. The question of the
development of Black's King's Bishop is of such importance
that it governs the two main lines of defence. As a third
example, we give the Wing Gambit.

(a) KING'S FIANCHETTO BY BLACK

1.	P—K4	P—QB4
2.	Kt—KB3	Kt—QB3

QUESTION 32. What should be the reply to 2. P—QB4 ?

3.	P—Q4	P×P
4.	Kt×P	P—KKt3

If Black first plays 4. .... Kt—KB3, then 5. Kt—QB3,
P—KKt3 ; 6. Kt×Kt, KtP×Kt ; 7. P—K5, Kt—Kt1 ;
8. Q—B3, B—KKt2 ; 9. B—QB4, etc. Much better in this
variation is 5. .... P—Q3 ; 6. B—K2, P—KKt3 ; 7. B—K3,
B—Kt2 ; 8. O—O, O—O ; etc. Thus one prevents the two
pawn advances by White to QB4 and K5.

5.	P—QB4	

A very important move, as we have already explained.
After this move White's position is very sound.

5.	....	B—Kt2
6.	Kt—Kt3	

Better than 6. B—K3, Kt—B3 ; 7. Kt—QB3, Kt—KKt5.

6.	....	Kt—B3
7.	Kt—B3	P—Q3
8.	B—K2	O—O
9.	B—K3	B—K3

with even chances.

(b) PAULSEN'S DEFENCE

1.	P—K4	P—QB4
2.	Kt—KB3	

QUESTION 33. How should the game be continued if
White renounces the move 3. P—Q4 and plays, for example,
2. Kt—QB3, followed by P—KKt3, B—Kt2, P—Q3, etc. ?

2.	....	P—K3
3.	P—Q4	P×P
4.	Kt×P	Kt—KB3

A good alternative for Black is 4. .... P—QR3, followed by 5. Kt—QB3, Q—B2 ; 6. B—K2, Kt—QB3 ; 7. O—O, P—Q3.

5.	Kt—QB3	P—Q3

After 5. .... B—Kt5, White could obtain an excellent game by 6. P—K5, Kt—K5 ; 7. Q—Kt4.

6.	B—K2	

Or even 6. B—Q3, with the idea of playing later on O—O, P—KB4, Q—B3, etc.

6.	....	B—K2
7.	O—O	O—O
8.	K—R1	P—QR3

with an even game.

(c) THE WING GAMBIT

1.	P—K4	P—QB4
2.	P—QKt4	

The idea is to draw the Queen's Bishop's pawn away from the centre. Out on the flank and constantly attacked, it will be worthless.

2.	....	P×P
3.	P—QR3	P—Q4

It would be bad for Black to capture the pawn, *e. g.*, 3. .... P×P ; 4. Kt×P, P—Q4 ; 5. P×P, Q×P ; 6. B—Kt2, but the following line is quite playable : 3. .... P—K4 ; 4. P×P, B×P ; 5. P—QB3, B—K2, etc.

4.	P—K5	Kt—QB3
5.	P—Q4	Q—B2
6.	Kt—KB3	B—Kt5

A very interesting position.

CENTRE COUNTER

(1. P—K4, P—Q4)

This defence is reminiscent of the Centre Game, which we have already analysed, and it has the same drawbacks. For though it is true that Black attacks the unprotected

King's pawn with his defended pawn, the immediate exchange brings his Queen to the middle of the board with all the risks that such a sortie implies. We have already pointed them out in the Centre Game. Here White has the further advantage of the move, and this makes itself felt all the more. Black can, of course, attempt to win back the pawn by means of another piece, but this cannot be done without appreciably increasing White's advantage in time.

From all points of view the use of this opening is to be discouraged, for it will give no advantage to Black, who will frequently have trouble in equalising. So he must resign himself to a purely passive game with the satisfaction of having exchanged a centre pawn, or he must continue to attack the enemy by opening up the game more. In the first case we already know the line of play to follow and Black's being a move behind will not make his task easier.

Let us now see what can be obtained from an attack, whose dangers we can estimate in advance.

Suppose that after 1. P—K4, P—Q4 ; 2. P×P, Q×P ; 3. Kt—QB3, Black plays 3. .... Q—K4 ch, the game will be continued with 4. B—K2, B—Kt5 ; 5. P—Q4, Q—K3 ; 6. B—K3, B×B ; 7. KKt×B. Now let us examine the position. All White's minor pieces have been brought out, while Black's only piece in play is his Queen, which occupies a dangerous position on the King's file. Evidently the Queen's retreat to K4 at the third move was not a happy choice ; let us try another one, say to QR4. After 4. P—Q4 let us carry out the attack in the same way as before, 4. .... P—K4 ; 5. P×P, B—QKt5 (5. .... Q×P ch will lead to the variations we have just seen) ; 6. B—Q2, Q×P ch ; 7. B—K2, B—Kt5 ; 8. P—KR3, B×B ; 9. KKt×B, and again White's superiority in development is obvious. This line of play is so inferior that White can even play 5. Kt—B3, simply to add to his advantage in development.

Black must therefore abandon the move 4. .... P—K4. After 1. P—K4, P—Q4 ; 2. P×P, Q×P ; 3. Kt—QB3, Q—QR4 ; 4. P—Q4, let us choose a quieter game, e.g., 4. .... Kt—KB3 ; 5. Kt—B3, P—B3 (5. .... B—Kt5 would not be bad, although after 6. P—KR3, B—R4 Black would have lost too much time in retreating both his pieces) ; 6. Kt—K5, B—B4 ; 7. B—Q3, B×B ; 8. Q×B, QKt—Q2 ;

9. P—B4, and White exerts a strong pressure in the centre.

The inferiority of these variations arises from the loss of time occasioned by the sortie of the Queen. Let us try to recapture the pawn with another piece. After 1. P—K4, P—Q4 ; 2. P×P, Black can play 2. .... Kt—KB3 to regain the pawn with his Knight. It would not be wise for White to hold on to his pawn by 3. P—QB4, for after 3. .... P—B3 ; 4. P×P, Kt×P Black obtains too great an advantage owing to the retarded development of White's Queen's pawn. White may, however, try 3. B—Kt5 ch. There follows 3. .... B—Q2 ; 4. B—B4, but Black can always win back his pawn as follows : 4. .... B—KKt5 ; 5. P—KB3, B—B4 ; 6. Kt—K2, Kt×P. It is better for White not to attempt to defend the pawn, but to allow Black to lose time in recapturing it, while White carries out his normal development, e. g., 3. P—Q4 Kt×P ; 4. Kt—KB3, or even 4. P—QB4.

To sum up, White in all cases is much ahead of Black in development. The positions may become equalised in the continuation and Black may even obtain an attack by O—O—O thanks to the opening of the Queen's file (an advantage of the Centre Counter over the Centre Game— White's Queen's pawn is weak). But it should always be possible to turn White's superiority to account in this opening.

ALEKHINE'S DEFENCE

(1. P—K4, KT—KB3)

Alekhine's Defence is one of the most modern types of opening and of quite recent invention. Although it is found, in essence at least, among some of the older games, the strategic system it exhibits bears quite an original stamp. As a matter of fact, it would be better placed with the modern openings than among the half-open games on account of the ideas it has in common with them.

It is also a most peculiar opening, for it seems to run counter to all the principles of sound and logical development. After the natural moves 1. P—K4, Kt—KB3 ; 2. P—K5, Kt—Q4 ; 3. P—QB4, Kt—Kt3 ; 4. P—Q4 we reach the position in the following diagram.

NO. 29. POSITION AFTER WHITE'S 4TH MOVE

Black has developed no other piece but his Knight, which has already made three consecutive moves and has merely reached a disadvantageous position.

White, on the other hand, has completely occupied the centre, has advanced three pawns without loss of time and always with a direct threat.

But just because these pawns are too far advanced and cannot be defended by other pawns, they demand constant protection and prove, in the long run, to be very weak. White's advance is gradually neutralised by repeated attacks on these pawns. What we have said about the backward centre and of the dangers of too rapid an advance, is clearly illustrated here. Further, we see the triumph of the principle of the general plan, in which it is not a particular move that counts, but the whole series of moves forming a complete strategical plan. The Knight moves to Kt3 not really to occupy that square but to weaken White's pawns and afterwards to attack them, e.g., 4. .... P—Q3 ; 5. P—B4, P×P ; 6. BP×P, Kt—B3. It is now Black who is developing his pieces with direct threats and without loss of time in doing so. How can white defend his King's pawn ? If he plays 7. Kt—KB3, Black replies with 7. .... B—Kt5 ; and if 8. B—K2, B×Kt ; 9. B×B, then 9. .... Kt×BP.

Beware ! A very simple trap.

After 9. B×B, Black must not play 9. .... Q×P, because he will lose his Queen by 10. B×Kt, ch.

White must therefore defend his pawn by 7. B—K3 and then we are faced with a very unusual state of affairs. It is the pieces which now defend the pawns and not the reverse, which would be the normal thing. Pieces are mobile troops and if they are kept back behind advanced pawns we cannot say that they have been "developed," for this term means nothing less than playing the pieces in front of the pawns. The premature pawn advance brings White near to the hostile front but does not develop his pieces. Black now redoubles his attacks, *e.g.*, 7. B—K3, B—B4 ; 8. Kt—QB3, P—K3 ; 9. B—K2, Kt—Kt5 ; 10. R—B1, P—B4. One feels already that White's centre will have to be given up. Black, as we learned in the French Defence, has still the move P—B3 in reserve to break down completely this fortress so imprudently erected too close to the enemy lines.

Let us apply the precepts that have been of such service in the French Defence and look at White's resources. In the first place he can exchange pawns at Q6 (*e.g.*, 1. P—K4, Kt—KB3 ; 2. P—K5, Kt—Q4 ; 3. P—QB4, Kt—Kt3 ; 4. P—Q4, P—Q3 ; 5. P×P), to avoid difficulties and to preserve his freedom of action. Again, he can even leave the Kt at Q4 and be satisfied with a normal game by playing 3. P—Q4, P—Q3 ; 4. P×P, KP×P ; 5. Kt—KB3, B—Kt5 ; 6. B—K2, B—K2 ; 7. O—O, O—O ; 8. R—K1, leaving a position which has none of the characteristics of Alekhine's Defence but is simply a formation in White's favour. But even in the first variation, where the four pawns are advanced, he can simplify the game by not allowing Black's Knight to move to Kt5, *i.e.*, by playing 8. P—QR3 after 7. .... B—B4. Finally, he can accept the whole variation just as we have given it, for it is not yet won by Black.

To sum up, all that White has to avoid in Alekhine's Defence is faulty judgment in thinking that he can obtain the better game by advancing his four centre pawns.

There are several ways of playing this defence. By way of example we give below the opening moves of a game recently played.

1.	P—K4	Kt—KB3
2.	P—K5	Kt—Q4
3.	P—QB4	Kt—Kt3
4.	P—Q4	P—Q3

5.	P—B4	P×P
6.	BP×P	Kt—B3
7.	B—K3	B—B4
8.	Kt—QB3	P—K3
9.	B—K2	B—K2
10.	Kt—B3	O—O
11.	O—O	P—B3
12.	Kt—KR4	P×P
13.	Kt×B	P×Kt
14.	P—Q5	Kt—Q5
15.	B×Kt	P×B
16.	Q×P	Kt—Q2
17.	K—R1	

and White preserves a slight advantage.

We are now in a position to tackle the ultra-modern openings. The Queen's Pawn Game with its strong and weak squares and its Queen-centre, and the half-open games with their backward centres and the struggle between different centres, have already brought us into contact with the elements which make up these very complex openings.

FOURTH GROUP

MODERN OPENINGS

Having analysed the openings in our first three groups, we have now reached the ultra-modern openings, which are the most difficult to understand. But, above all, these openings, though entirely different in character from those previously studied, do not disown the older principles. Let us briefly recall them.

To start with, we learned the five general rules which govern all openings more or less rigorously, but particularly the open games. Then we came to recognise the existence of strong and weak squares, which guided us so much in the close games and which will be just as important in the modern openings. Finally, we studied the first ideas concerning the backward centre and their corollaries about the dangers of the advanced centre. Now modern openings separate themselves into two main groups : (1) A backward centre by Black opposed to a Queen-centre by White, (2) A backward centre on both sides. Consequently we must now specially enlarge upon the uses and characteristics of the backward centre when opposed either to another backward centre or to an advanced centre.

Let us briefly repeat the complaints made against the advanced centre, whether it is a King's or a Queen's. For what solid reasons is a passive centre—which seems to contradict the rule of occupying the centre—preferred to an advanced centre ? Also, what shall we say about two backward centres—which give the appearance that both sides are playing a defensive game—when we have spoken of White's initiative in the centre and of Black's attempts to obtain possession of it ? It is simply that we have progressed during the study of this book. Experience, and above all, examples from actual play, have demonstrated the inferiority of the advanced and prematurely-occupied centre. Firstly, occupation of the advanced centre frequently leads to numerous exchanges, which simplify the game to such an extent that there is no longer any chance of advantage,

especially as one's opponent himself succeeds in building up
a centre with comparative ease.   Further, effective occupation of the centre is not easy.   Pieces are often driven away
or exchanged, equalising the chances of both opponents,
neither one nor the other being able to point to any superiority.
The result is that their respective advantages are limited to
the occupation of one or two squares to no appreciable profit.

Finally, the premature occupation of an advanced centre
makes it weak, as the pawns thus exposed become the targets
of hostile attacks.   A solitary White pawn at K4 provides
the first example of this weakness and both Alekhine's
Defence and the French Defence have shown the dangers
of a central formation of advanced pawns, preventing the
development of the pieces.

There is also the psychological factor.   As a rule it is a
good thing to conceal one's intentions as long as possible and
not to be too deeply committed too soon to one line of play.
An advanced centre produces exactly the opposite effect.
Maintenance of the centre is its whole business, for the
centre will be the base of offensive operations, so that our
strategical plan holds no secrets from our opponent, who
will be able to prepare a satisfactory defence at his leisure.
To say dogmatically, "Do not occupy the centre until you
have developed all your pieces," would be to go against all
the accepted principles and would obviously be wrong, for
we have never stated that the occupation of the centre in-
evitably leads to the loss of the game.   All that we have just
said simply goes to show that we must not be satisfied with
an opening which simplifies the game too much and that
there are some players whose imagination demands more
complications and who prefer a slow and subtle game to a
premature hand-to-hand conflict.

Above all, do not run away with the idea that ultra-modern
openings deny the importance of the centre.   On the contrary.   Its occupation is delayed so that it may be permanent
and effective.   Thus it can be said that the essential idea of
these openings is always the centre, whose permanent establishment requires some preparation as, for example, the
fianchetto of the Bishop, a method commonly used.   It has
often been advanced as a "principle" that both Knights must
be brought out before the Bishops, but this is at variance
with all the openings.   This false "principle" is accounted

for as follows : A Knight must make two moves before it
reaches a square where it threatens the enemy position,
while the Bishop is a long-range piece and can attack from
a distance, and if it ventures into the enemy camp it is easily
repulsed. It can, therefore, produce a lasting effect along
an open diagonal while sheltering behind its own pawns.

When one plays one's Bishop to Kt2, one does not by this
move give up the occupation of the centre, nor does one
restrict oneself to an attack on the opposite wing. One
occupies the long diagonal to keep the centre under observation and to prepare for its occupation. The Bishop at
KKt2 has further advantages. It defends the castled position strongly, so much so that frequently the opponent seeks
to exchange it by the well-known manœuvre Q—Q2 followed
by B—KR6. Furthermore, the observation of the centre
by no means confines the attention of the Bishop to one
wing more than to the other, for, if a Bishop developed
normally on a square near the centre cannot change its
direction without difficulty, one posted at Kt2, by virtue of
the long diagonal it commands, will be easily able to occupy
another diagonal directed against the other wing. This
change of direction evidently implies the complete command of the centre which becomes the "turn-table" of the
position. Summing up, we may say that modern openings
delay for a few moves the beginning of the struggle. In
the open game, battle is joined immediately, but in the
modern openings there is first of all a phase of preparation
for the battle. Without carrying immediate threats, the
opening moves conform to a general plan which determines
the squares on which this preparation is built up. Truly
this is the realisation of Capablanca's "general plan."

Thus the centre gains in importance, and the absolute
control of certain squares often decides the issue of the
game. These squares are not merely the strong and weak
squares referred to in the close openings but are still more
important. They may be called "critical" squares because
they are generally at the intersection of the lines of action
of several pieces and serve as the objective of all manœuvres.
Those who play the openings mechanically, without
recognising the importance of these "critical" squares,
must not be surprised to lose often without being able
to account for their inferiority. They do not make losing

moves, but they have missed the whole point of the opening.

A "critical" square serves as a pivot for the pieces which command it and this multiple control of it prevents hostile pawns from occupying it. As a general rule, however, it is the business of pieces rather than pawns to take possession of it. Call to mind the variation of the French Defence in which White's pawns at Q4 and K5 have been exchanged. These two squares are first observed, and then occupied by White's pieces.

Similarly in modern openings, the "critical" squares are first controlled and observed and then occupied by pieces. The critical square K4, for example, serves as the pivot for the manœuvres in Monticelli's famous trap.

After 1. P—Q4, Kt—KB3 ; 2. P—QB4, P—K3 ; 3. Kt—KB3, B—Kt5 ch ; 4. B—Q2, B×B ch ; 5. Q×B, P—QKt3 ; 6. P—KKt3, B—Kt2 ; 7. B—Kt2, O—O, 8. Kt—B3, Kt—K5, Black occupies the critical square, his K5, and to drive him from it White plays 9. Q—B2. If, now, Black plays 9 .... Kt×Kt ? (instead of P—KB4) the continuation 10. Kt—Kt5, Kt—K5 ; 11. B×Kt, B×B ; 12. Q×B wins the Exchange by the double attack on the Rook and on Black's King's Rook's pawn. This variation is a good example of the utilisation of a critical square. One after the other, White and Black pieces occupy it with various threats.

The following is an illustration of the change of direction of White's Bishop at the critical square, K4.

NO. 30. POSITION AFTER BLACK'S 14TH MOVE
(Alekhine *v.* Bogoljubov, Triberg Tournament, 1921)

In this position, in order to control his K4 and to avoid exchanging his King's Bishop, White plays 15. R×P, with the continuation, 15. .... Kt—Kt5 ; 16. B—K4 ! suddenly changing the direction of his attack and leading to a winning position, *e.g.*, 16. .... P—B4 ; 17. B×P, R×B ; 18. R—Q8 ch, etc.

Thus the Bishop, moving from Kt2 to K4, became the principal instrument in the attack on Black's KR2 !

So, as we have just seen, a critical square may assume an importance surpassing that of all the strong squares in a position. It must not be considered, however, to be entirely independent of such squares, for, on the contrary, these have brought critical squares into being around them. Actually we are brought face to face with a "family" of strong and weak squares influencing one another. Acting along the long diagonals, the Bishops in fianchetto tend particularly to create groups of strong and weak squares. It follows, of course, that the exchange or disappearance of these Bishops causes an immediate weakness on squares of the same colour. This weakening has repercussions right to the end of the game, and that is why, in modern openings, even more than in others, special attention must be given to the "pawn skeleton," in the absence of pieces. Let us now consider the following positions :

NO. 31. PAWN SKELETON AFTER BLACK'S 24TH MOVE
(Alekhine *v.* Znosko-Borovsky, Birmingham Tournament, 1926)

In the above position, Black's pawn formation is obviously inferior, as the pawns at his QB2 and Q3 do not form part of the principal pawn chain, and the pawn at K5 is too far advanced. Above all, however, it is the weakness of Black's Queen's Rook's pawn which makes itself felt, for it can be immediately attacked by the enemy, whereas White's Queen's Rook's pawn is beyond the reach of Black's King. Black can defend the pawn, but if White plays P—B5 Black will have only one square available for this purpose (his QR3), and, however he plays, the pawn will ultimately fall. If there are pieces left on the board, they may counterbalance this weakness of the pawns. It may, instead, be that they will increase it. In every case White's plan is a simple one. He will exchange some of the pieces to exploit the inferior pawn skeleton.

NO. 32.   PAWN SKELETON AFTER BLACK'S 11TH MOVE
(Alekhine *v*. Ibanez, Buenos Aires, 1926)

In this position White has a Queen-centre against Black's backward centre. Black's pawn skeleton has holes at his QR3, QB3 and KB3, and also a weak pawn at KR3. As long as he keeps his Bishops he can adequately defend these squares, but it follows that the Bishops will lose much of their offensive power as a result. On the other hand, White's position has only one hole, his KR3.

Altogether, in spite of having a backward centre, Black has made five pawn moves, while White, with an advanced

centre, has made but three. Thus, if we were considering
merely the pawn skeletons, the position of Black's pawns
is inferior to those of White's.

We can already conclude that the backward centre is a
very difficult weapon to handle, for while one can always
detect the direct threats of the enemy in the open games
and the tactical methods of attack and defence, the modern
openings rest more on the strategical plan of campaign.   The
carrying out of these strategical ideas is itself very delicate,
and the manœuvres differ in every position.   A backward
centre, as such, can be a disadvantage, and if it cannot at
a given moment be transformed into an advanced centre,
the immobility it imposes will be slowly stifling.   To place
a Bishop at Kt2 without any strategical idea is absolutely
senseless.   We shall therefore try to find out exactly how
a Bishop in fianchetto can act, because this frequently-
occurring formation is at the root of the chief differences
between the older openings and the modern ones.

Suppose White develops his Bishop at KKt2.   Black will
soon have to decide how to play in order to restrict the scope
of this piece.   We make no claim of giving the only methods
which will do so but we shall be content to bring forward,
by means of examples, a few possible considerations.

The first idea for counteracting a White Bishop at KKt2
is to oppose it with a Black Bishop at QKt2.   The action of
White's Bishop is thus neutralised by Black's Bishop controlling the same diagonal.   Exchange of Bishops may occur
and the simplified positions are liable to be drawn.   However, we must not jump to such a hasty conclusion, for the
pawn skeleton, although apparently symmetrical, gives White
an advantage in the end-game.   Clearly Black's weak squares,
QR3 and QB3, are farther from his King than are White's
KR3 and KB3 from *his* King, and to prevent a hostile piece
from occupying them, Black will have to use one of his
pieces for their defence alone.   White's first advantage thus
is an active piece against a passive one.

Moreover, for the end-game, White's pawn formation
(KR2, KKt3, KB2) is preferable to Black's (QR2, QKt3,
QB2).   The removal of the Bishops is also rather to White's
advantage, for in the middle game Black's Bishop at QKt2
attacks the castled position and plays, or at least ought to

play, an active part, while White's Bishop at KKt2 is limited to the defence of the castled position. The exchange of Bishops is not so profitable for White in the opening, for apart from the vulnerability of the castled position resulting from the absence of a Bishop at KKt2, the potential activity of this piece at K4, for example, in changing direction, must make White hesitate to exchange it. It is a much better plan to close the diagonal. If White does so by moving a pawn to K4, his Bishop's range on this diagonal will be much shorter (KR1—KB3) than that of Black's Bishop (QR1—K5); it is better, therefore, to close the diagonal at Q5 for then K4 may eventually serve as a pivot for the Bishop now at Kt2.

Evidently, by advancing a pawn to Q5 to close the long diagonal, we abandon to the enemy the squares QB5 and K5—excellent posts for a Knight—but we cannot have it all ways. On his side, Black will leave open the long diagonal by placing his central pawns on Black squares, and when the diagonal is closed by a White pawn at its Q5, he can either change the diagonal by playing B—QB1 to attack the castled King by B—R6, or he can defend his own castled position from an attack starting with the move B—K4 by playing P—KB4 or B—KB4. There is also the manœuvre B—R3, attacking the White Queen's Bishop's pawn which will probably move to QB4 in support of the pawn at Q5. As for occupying his QB4 with a Knight, Black must not forget to play the preventive move P—QR4, otherwise White will dislodge the Knight by P—QKt4.

To summarise, the most natural strategical plan to oppose White's development of his Bishop at KKt2 is based on the move B—QKt2 : we have already seen an example of this in Monticelli's Trap (p. 121).

A second plan to destroy the effectiveness of White's King's Bishop is to play P—QB3. This simple move protects the whole of Black's Queen's side against the pressure of the White Bishop and at the same time gives his own Bishop complete freedom of action.

Black can try to exchange Bishops at KR6 by the manœuvre B—K3, Q—Q2, and B—R6, but White has two ways of avoiding the exchange. He can play P—KR3 followed by K—R2, or R—K1 and, if B—R6, then B—R1.

We see, however, that in spite of its power on the long

diagonal, the freedom of Black's Bishop is somewhat restricted, for by the move P—QB3, he surrenders to White an important section of the diagonal (KR1 to Q5).

Besides, even on the diagonal QB1 to KR6, certain squares will be closed to the Black Bishop, for Black has yet to decide how he is going to develop the centre pawns. If, after P—QB3 he plays P—K3, his Queen's Bishop will be shut in ; if P—K4, his Queen's pawn will be weakened ; and finally if he keeps his King's pawn on its original square, he gives his opponent full liberty of action in the centre.

After P—QB3 there remains to consider the logical continuation P—Q4. Logical though it may appear, this move runs counter to the idea of consolidating the Queen's side, for the Queen's pawn will become the target of repeated attacks by White (e. g., P—QB4 and P—K4) and it will still have to be defended by P—K3.

We thus arrive at a position having a Queen-centre opposed to a King-centre instead of two backward centres. In this formation Black must guard his Q4 with his Queen's Bishop's pawn, to close a little more the long diagonal, while his pieces developed under the shelter of this pawn can move freely.

In conclusion, let us compare the results obtained from the two methods proposed for counteracting White's Bishop at KKt2.

In this last method, Black places his pawns on white squares to limit the scope of the White Bishop, but renders them more open to attack. In the first plan, Black places his pawns on black squares so as to give the White Bishop nothing to attack, but allows it complete freedom of action along the long diagonal. We should add here that the relation of colour between the squares occupied by our pawns and the hostile Bishop can also have very serious consequences in both the middle and the end-game.

In the two plans we have just explained for counteracting a Bishop occupying a long diagonal, we first investigated the opposition of the Bishops on the same diagonal, and then the displacement of the defensive Bishop to a parallel diagonal.

There is a third way to operate against such a fianchetto. Instead of opposing our Bishop of the same colour on the same diagonal, we leave this diagonal to our opponent and develop our Bishop of the opposite colour at its Kt2. Thus we have a contest between Bishops of opposite colours on

the two long diagonals. Further, our whole system of
development must be altered. All our pieces must support
our Bishop and then we shall see whose Bishop is the stronger.
Now, if we develop our Bishop thus but do not accept the
obligation in development it imposes, we may make good
moves and yet lose the game, because at some time or other
our opponent's Bishop, supported by all his pieces suitably
developed, will be stronger than our unsupported Bishop.

That is the difficulty in playing modern openings. We
deal not with immediate threats but with broad strategical
plans, and these must be understood clearly before we can
play the openings well.

Here, then, we see that the diagonals where the struggle
takes place cross each other though the Bishops never actually
meet or control the same squares as they do when they are
opposed along the same diagonal.

It is, however, possible for Bishops of the same colour
to be posted on diagonals which cross each other at right
angles and this type of action is a rather curious example of
the struggle against a Bishop in fianchetto.

The following position is an illustration of this form of
counter-action in which the Black Bishop, in fianchetto,
controls the open long diagonal, while the White Bishop,
instead of opposing it or commanding a parallel diagonal,
counter-attacks in a direction at right angles.

NO. 33. POSITION AFTER BLACK'S 26TH MOVE
(Znosko-Borovsky *v.* Tartakover, Paris Tournament, 1930)

The game was continued as follows : 27. P—Q5, P—Kt3 ; 28. B—B4, K—B2 ; 29. Q—R2, Q—K1 ; 30. Q—Kt3, P—B3 ; 31. P×P ch, P×P ; 32. B×P ch !, K—Kt2 ; 33. P—Kt4, P×P ; 34 P—B5 ! P×P ; 35 Kt×P ch, and White won.

As we see, the decision was not obtained on the long diagonal nor on one parallel to it, but on lines which crossed it at right angles. The non-participation of the Black Bishop in the defence made the attack irresistible.

The different ideas that we have just expressed give a fairly accurate idea of the problems which have to be solved in the modern openings. Instead of direct threats we find strategical ideas ; instead of exchanges in the centre we have the backward centre ; instead of a weak square we have a whole series of weaknesses ; instead of simple development of the pieces we play to prevent the possibility of hostile action. In general, we see the importance of open lines.

The opening of lines is to the advantage of the stronger side, and more particularly if they are opened at the point where the strength lies. If one has the inferior game, one should avoid opening lines, especially those bearing upon the weak points of the position. We have just seen the value of the long diagonals and in the open game we often had occasion to emphasise the importance of open files. It now remains for us to say a few words about the ranks, whose occupation doubles the power of a Rook. A sudden pressure along a rank is the more dangerous because our "front" is not in the least prepared for this sort of battle. In attack, this lateral action is often sufficient to decide the issue of a hitherto inconclusive contest, while in defence the Rook can act at long range and so become even more effective.

In the centre of the board a Rook can attack pieces and pawns on both wings or can be rapidly moved along a decisive file, and we already know that the mobility of a Rook is a very important factor in winning an end-game. But it is above all on the 7th rank that a Rook exerts its greatest power, for the enemy pawns on it are not supported by other pawns : also if there are few pawns there to threaten, the power of the Rook is felt at a greater distance and can even be used to co-operate on a direct attack on the hostile King.

We point out, in passing, that this manœuvre takes place in two stages. First comes the occupation of an open file, and secondly, the use of it to reach an advantageous traverse.

We give three examples to illustrate what we have just said. We shall not dilate upon the function of the rank in defence, for everyone has been able to assess its value by his own experience.

NO. 34. POSITION AFTER WHITE'S 25TH MOVE
(Nimzowitsch *v.* Capablanca, New York Tournament, 1927)

The continuation was: 25. .... R—B7; 26. Q—R6, P—K4; 27. B×KP, R(Q1)—Q7; 28. Q—Kt7, R×P; 29. P—Kt4, Q—K3; 30. B—Kt3, R×P; 31. Q—B3, R(R7)—Kt7 ch; 32. Q×R, R×Q ch; 33. K×R, Q×KtP, and Black won.

NO. 35. POSITION AFTER WHITE'S 27TH MOVE
(Nimzowitsch *v.* Capablanca, New York Tournament, 1927)

The play was as follows : 27. .... R—B5 ; 28. Q—R3,
K—Kt2 ; 29. R—KB2, P—R4 ; 30. R—K2, Kt—B4 ;
31. Kt×Kt ch, KtP×Kt ; 32. Q—B3, K—Kt3 ; 33. R(K2)
—Q2, R—K5 ; 34. R—Q4, R—B5 ; 35. Q—B2, Q—Kt4 ;
36. K—Kt3, R(B5)×R ; 37. P×R, Q—B5 ; 38. K—Kt2,
P—Kt4 ; 39. K—Kt1, P—Kt5 ; 40. P×P, P×P ; 41. K—Kt2,
Q—B8 ; 42. K—Kt3, Q—KR8 ; 43. R—Q3, R—K8 ;
44. R—KB3, R—Q8 ; 45. P—Kt3, R—QB8 ; 46. R—K3,
R—B8 ; and Black won.

In No. 34 Black obtains two Rooks on the 7th rank by
sacrificing a pawn (one might well sacrifice more to obtain
such an advantage), while in No. 35 Black begins by occupying his 5th rank, and when he has reduced all White's pieces
to the defensive, he wins the game quickly on the 8th rank.

No. 36 is a perfect illustration of the combined action of
diagonals, files and ranks.   There is also an isolated pawn
which is sacrificed to open the long diagonals for the Bishops.
The Black Rook eventually occupies the 7th rank, and aided
by the two Bishops, hastens the decision in a position which
a few moves before had appeared to be in favour of White.

NO. 36.   POSITION AFTER WHITE'S 19TH MOVE
(Biscay v. Znosko-Borovsky, Paris, 1932)

The game continued : 19. .... P—QR4 ; 20. R—Kt1,
P×P ; 21. P×P, R—R7 ; 22. K—R1, R—K5 ; 23. Kt—K2,
P—Q5 ! ; 24. K—Kt1, R—K1 ; 25. R—R3, Q—Q4 ; 26. K—B1,

Q—R8 ch ; 27. Kt—Kt1, R—K6 ; 28. R×R, P×R ; 29. Q×P,
Q—Kt7 ch ; 30. K—K1, R×P ! and wins.

It may appear that we have deviated from our subject.
But the fact is that modern openings, as much as but not more
than others, provide a setting for the use of open lines.
However, preparation for the opening of lines forms part of
the strategical and slowly-developed ideas which are the
essential characteristics of the modern openings.

We can now pass on to the definite application of the various
principles just explained, and to this end we shall divide
modern openings into two distinct groups : (A) An ordinary
centre opposed to a backward centre (a) without fianchetto,
(b) with the King's fianchetto, (c) with the Queen's fianchetto.
(B) A contest between two backward centres.

(A) A BACKWARD CENTRE AGAINST A QUEEN-CENTRE
(1. P—Q4, KT—KB3 ; 2. P—QB4, P—K3)

In this group of openings White plays the Queen's Gambit
or Queen's Pawn Game and Black replies with a backward
centre without resorting to the fianchetto of his Bishops, at
least in the early stages of his development. Already the
advance of White's pawns to the centre has created a weakness at K4. So Black strives to occupy it with a piece and
to make this square an advanced post for his operations.
This threat makes White change the usual course of the
Queen's Pawn Game in order to prevent his opponent from
achieving his object, or, if he permits the occupation of
his K4, he will multiply his attacks on this square. Frequently,
too, White castles QR, and exposes himself to a strong attack
on the somewhat weakened Queen's side. Black, on the
other hand, thanks to his almost unassailable backward
centre, is ready to withstand no matter what attacks, and to
counter-attack at any part of the board.

NIMZOWITSCH'S VARIATION

1.	P—Q4	Kt—KB3
2.	P—QB4	P—K3
3.	Kt—QB3	B—Kt5
4.	Q—B2	

Another continuation is 4. Q—Kt3, P—B4 ; 5. P×P,
Kt—B3 ; 6. Kt—B3 (if 6. B—Q2, then 6 .... B×P ;

7. P—K3, O—O; 8. Kt—B3, P—Q4; 9. B—K2, etc.)
Kt—K5 (if 6. .... B×P; then 7. B—Kt5); 7. B—Q2,
Kt×B; 8. Kt×Kt, P—B4, to prevent the Knight going to
K4.

QUESTION 34. If in the above variation Black happened
to play Kt—Q5, why could not the Queen take the Bishop?

4.	P—B4

The move 4. .... P—Q4 would transpose into a Queen's
Pawn Game.

5.	P×P	Kt—B3
6.	Kt—B3	B×P
7.	B—Kt5	B—K2
8.	P—K4	

If White plays 8. O—O—O, then 8. .... Q—R4;
9. P—QR3, P—QR3; 10. P—K3, P—QKt3 would be
dangerous to him.

8.	....	Q—R4
9.	B—Q2	Q—B2
10.	B—K2	P—QR3

A position full of possibilities.

<h3 style="text-align:center">BOGOLJUBOV'S VARIATION</h3>

1.	P—Q4	Kt—KB3
2.	P—QB4	P—K3
3.	Kt—KB3	B—Kt5 ch

The Blumenfeld Gambit gives Black attacking chances,
e.g., 3. .... P—B4; 4. P—Q5, P—QKt4; and White should
not win a pawn by 5. QP×P because of 5. .... BP×P;
6. P×P, P—Q4, giving Black a strong centre and the attack.
A better move for White is 5. B—Kt5.

4.	B—Q2	B×B ch
5.	Q×B	P—QKt3
6.	Kt—B3	B—Kt2
7.	P—KKt3	O—O
8.	B—Kt2	Kt—K5

Here 8. .... P—Q3, with the idea of continuing with
P—K4, would be too passive. To carry out this plan, it
should have been already prepared by 4. .... Q—K2.

9.	Q—B2	P—KB4

By playing 9. .... Kt×Kt, Black would fall into the Monticelli trap, as we have already seen (p. 121).

    10. Kt—K5   P—Q4

Black has not even been able to build up a backward centre and finds himself obliged to resort to a too open one.

    11. P×P   P×P
    12. O—O   Kt—Q2

White has the better game.

QUEEN'S FIANCHETTO DEFENCE

    1. P—Q4   Kt—KB3
    2. P—QB4   P—K3

The Budapest Counter-Gambit is quite playable here, *e.g.*, 2. .... P—K4 ; 3. P×P, Kt—Kt5 ; and White will do better to concentrate on a rapid development by 4. P—K4 than to defend the pawn by 4. P—B4.

    3. Kt—KB3   P—QKt3
    4. Kt—B3

By playing 4. P—KKt3, B—Kt2 ; 5. B—Kt2, B—Kt5 ch, we return to Bogoljubow's Variation, but Black can avoid it in part by playing 5. .... P—B4 ; 6. P—Q5, P×P ; 7. Kt—KR4, P—Kt3, etc. It is therefore better for Black to play B—Kt2 before checking at Kt5 with the Bishop.

    4. ....   B—Kt2
    5. Q—B2   P—B4

Having obtained control of his K5 by the Knight at B3, Black by this move attacks the White pawn at Q4 and "opens" the game.

    6. P—K4   P×P
    7. Kt×P   P—Q3
    8. B—K2   B—K2
    9. B—K3   O—O
    10. O—O   QKt—Q2
    11. KR—Q1   P—QR3

White has a slightly better game than Black.

QUESTION 35. What other opening does this variation recall ?

KING'S FIANCHETTO DEFENCE

    1. P—Q4   Kt—KB3
    2. P—QB4   P—KKt3
    3. Kt—QB3   B—Kt2
    4. P—K4

The following continuation gives White a more solid
position : 4. Kt—B3, O—O ; 5. P—K4, P—Q3 ; 6. B—K2,
B—Kt5 ; 7. B—K3, etc.

4.	O—O
5. P—B4	

This advance of the four central pawns is as dangerous as
it is tempting.   5. B—K3, P—Q3 ; 6. P—B3, Kt—B3
would be more solid.

5.	P—Q3
6. Kt—B3	P—B4
7. P—Q5	

After 7. P×P Black would obtain a good game by 7. ....
Q—R4 ; 8. P×P, Kt×P ; 9. P×P, R—K1, etc.

7.	P—K3
8. B—K2	

8. B—Q3 would be worse, for after 8. .... P×P ; 9. BP×P,
Q—Kt3 ; 10. B—B2, P—B5 ; 11. Q—K2, R—K1, Black
would exert strong pressure on the centre (Colle v. Euwe,
Rotterdam, 1926).

8.	P×P
9. BP×P	P—QR3

Black has quite a good game.

In all these variations Black's move Kt—KB3, played
very early, is very important as it commands the two squares
Q4 and K5.   P—QB4 is also very useful to him as it attacks
the Queen's pawn.   We shall not be surprised to find White
making use of the same methods when he does not wish to
build up an advanced centre.

Now let us pass on to a backward centre by White.   In
the first example Black opposes it by an advanced centre and
opens the Queen's file ; in the second we see a battle between
two backward centres.

(a) BACKWARD CENTRE (WHITE) v. ADVANCED CENTRE (BLACK)

1. Kt—KB3	

After 1. P—QB4 Black has the choice between the replies
given to 1. Kt—KB3 and the move 1. .... P—K4 which
leads to a very open game, e.g., 1. .... P—K4 ; 2. Kt—QB3,
Kt—QB3 ; 3. Kt—B3, Kt—B3 ; 4. P—Q4, etc.

1.	P—Q4
2. P—B4	

The Réti Gambit. The move 2. P—K4 gives the Tenison Gambit. More positional moves, *e.g.*, 2. P—KKt3, 2. P—QKt3 or 2. P—K3, can, instead, be played.

2.	....	P×P
3.	Kt—R3	P—K4

Alternative and quieter moves are 3. .... Kt—KB3, 3. .... P—QB4 and 3. .... P—QR3.

4.	Kt×KP	B×Kt
5.	Q—R4 ch	P—QKt4

A trap. White cannot take this pawn as he will lose a piece, *e.g.*, 6. Q×P ch, P—B3 ; 7. Kt×QBP, Kt×Kt ; 8. Q×Kt ch, B—Q2 ; 9. Q—K4 ch, B—K2.

6.	Q×B	B—Kt2

Better would be 6. .... Q—Q4 ; 7. Q—KB3, Kt—KB3 ; 8. Q×Q, Kt×Q ; 9. P—KKt3, P—KB3 ; 10. B—Kt2, B—Kt2, etc. (Kashdan *v.* Nimzowitsch, Veldes (Bled) Tournament, 1931).

7.	P—K3	

7. P—QKt3 leads to a pretty little trap, *e.g.*, 7. .... Q—Q3 ; 8. B—Kt2 ?, P—B6 !, winning a piece.

7.	....	Q—Q3
8.	Q×Q	P×Q
9.	Kt—B3	Kt—QB3
10.	P—QKt3	P—Q4
11.	P×P	QP×P
12.	P—QR4	

White has the better game.

One can play very much the same variation without sacrificing a pawn, and a game of a more modern type results.

1.	Kt—KB3	Kt—KB3
2.	P—QB4	P—K3
3.	P—KKt3	P—Q4
4.	P—Kt3	P—B4
5.	B—KKt2	Kt—B3
6.	O—O	B—K2
7.	P—Q3	O—O
8.	B—Kt2	P—Q5
9.	P—K4	

White has the advantage (Capablanca *v.* Marshall, Moscow Tournament, 1925).

QUESTION 36.   How should Black decline the Réti Gambit ?
Why is 2. .... P—Q5 bad after 1. Kt—KB3, P—Q4 ;
2. P—B4 ?

(B)   TWO BACKWARD CENTRES

When we decide to build up a backward centre, we should
not feel obliged to keep it intact for the whole of the game.

Our opponent would then have at his disposal all the
important central squares and would gradually increase a
pressure which would end by literally stifling our game.

On the contrary, we must be thinking about the advance
of this backward centre from the moment when all our
pieces are developed, or even before that, if our opponent
weakens his position by premature advances.

Thus the important thing is to be able to choose the
opportune moment to transform this backward centre into
an advanced centre, for this second step will give us control
of all the important squares and may decide the issue.

(a)

1.	Kt—KB3	Kt—KB3
2.	P—B4	P—QKt3
3.	P—KKt3	B—Kt2
4.	B—Kt2	P—B4
5.	O—O	P—Kt3
6.	P—Q3	B—Kt2
7.	Kt—B3	O—O
8.	B—Q2	P—Q3
9.	R—Kt1	QKt—Q2
10.	P—QKt4	Q—B1
11.	Q—B1	P—Q4

and Black frees his game (Tartakower v. Müller, Bardfelt
Tournament, 1926).

(b)

1.	Kt—KB3	Kt—KB3
2.	P—B4	P—K3
3.	P—KKt3	P—QKt3
4.	B—Kt2	B—Kt2
5.	O—O	B—K2
6.	Kt—B3	O—O
7.	P—QR3	P—B4
8.	P—Q3	P—Q4
9.	Kt—K5	Q—B1

Here it is Black who first advances to the centre (Nagy
v. Kmoch, Debreczin Tournament, 1925).

We feel that we can now leave our reader to his own
initiative. We have studied examples of all the principal
openings, and we venture to hope that he is ready to face
the many variations presented to him in the course of a game.

Let him recall our "leit-motiv" : Chess is not an exercise
of memory ; one can, and should, understand the openings,
without learning variations by heart.

CONCLUSION

We have now reached the end of our journey. While
making no claim that we have exhausted the subject, we
have, instead of merely enumerating variations, tried to
examine thoroughly their basic ideas, in order to extract
from them the general principles by which the opening of
any game of chess is governed.

Noting the evolution of these ideas in the course of this
book, we have been led to point out such radical changes
that the reader may have noticed contradictions in it. The
closed centre has replaced the open centre, the advanced
centre has given way to the backward centre. Territorial
gain has seemed to be a disadvantage and rapid development
itself has lost its pre-eminence with the realisation of the
latent power of the pieces. The Bishops, too, have become
cautious and take cover behind their pawns rather than
venture into open country.

Thus, the principles laid down at the beginning of
this work seem to inspire less reverence as we progress
to the modern openings. Even the appreciation of gain
of material is not unaffected by these changes ; after
having recklessly sacrificed in the Gambits to obtain a
direct attack, we discovered that to be a pawn ahead was
enough to win a game, a fact which condemned Gambits.
Then the danger of capturing a pawn in the opening quickly
showed itself with experience and we came to regard the
gain of a pawn in the opening as delaying development and
compromising the game. And, finally, here we are, to-day,
witnessing the revival of most unusual gambits, in which a
pawn is sacrificed not merely for the sake of a strong attack,

but for a mere positional advantage. Everything has been upset; even the famous dictum, "A Knight at QKt3 is always badly placed," has been refuted in Alekhine's Defence. However, let us keep to the point and make use of this last example. An isolated case or an exception like this does not invalidate a general rule, which may suffer amendment without affecting its general applicability. Let us recapitulate the primary truths which have resisted the onslaughts of time and fashion. Although a Knight is sometimes stronger than a Rook, the latter still remains the superior piece, and a Queen is still stronger than a pawn, even though there may be occasions when a pawn wins against a Queen.

Similarly, central squares are and remain the most important on the board, and their occupation retains all its value. A good development is better than a bad one, and a large number of pieces in action can never be balanced by a limited number, etc. Actually we have learnt only the value of finesse; but it should not cause us to overlook essentials, and we must not overdo it. The desire to be too clever leads us to ineffective finesse.

Perhaps we shall never be able to solve the question as to whether the initial position is ripe for the commencement of operations or whether it should undergo transformations by preparatory manoeuvres; the temperament and style of the player will more often decide that point than reason or logic.

The openings of to-day are imbued with the modern spirit. Instead of bayonet charges and cavalry raids, we have trench warfare.

The resemblance goes farther than that: if we see, from day to day, new achievements in chess showing a greater desire for adventure, we see a revival of imagination and inspiration side by side with it. The name of the World's Champion alone calls to mind the deepest creations of the imagination.

This tendency in the opening finds its best interpreter of all in Alekhine: initiative before everything else. Neglecting mechanical development for a while, we can sometimes by direct threats, impose on our opponent some inferior formation. Development, provisionally suspended by both sides (and therefore without disadvantage) is afterwards

taken up again with more precision when the skeleton of the
game has already taken shape as a result of preliminary
manœuvres. In the introduction, we spoke of the advantages
of having the initiative for the development of the pieces :
here it is a question of another kind of initiative based on
tactical possibilities. For, to sum up, a game of chess is not
only the methodical application of strategic principles ;
tactical issues have an important place. Tactics are governed
by imagination and throw in relief the personal qualities of
the player during the game. These early attacks must,
however, always be prompted by favourable tactical
possibilities.

Take for example the Ruy Lopez. After 1. P—K4,
P—K4 ; 2. Kt—KB3, Kt—QB3 ; 3. B—Kt5, P—QR3 ;
4. B—R4, P—Q3 ; 5. O—O, Black has an opportunity of
taking the initiative by playing P—KKt4 because White's
King's Knight has no good retreat and White has already
castled on his King's side.

This tactical use of initiative is found again in the Wing
Gambit of the Sicilian Defence and in Blumenfeld's Counter
Gambit to the Queen's Gambit. It is always a matter of a
sudden advance on the flank carrying a direct threat or else
of a strengthening of the centre by drawing off hostile pieces
from this flank ; strategy based on tactics. For instance, let
us examine the position shown in the following diagram.

NO. 37.   POSITION AFTER WHITE'S 11TH MOVE
(Ahues *v.* Alekhine, San Remo Tournament, 1930)

It appears that no attack is possible for Black, for his pieces are in a purely passive formation and, besides, White has no weakness. However, Black, seizing a tactical opportunity, plays 11. .... P—Kt4, because White's Knight at B3 has no good retreat, and White cannot castle on the Queen's side on account of the open Knight's file. Further, this move has a positional object; the pawn at Kt4 will be used to support a Knight, which, eventually driven away from Q4, will be safely established at B5.

Thus we arrive at the conclusion that we can not only attack a weak position, but also weaken a position by attacking it.

Consider now the position in the following diagram.

NO. 38. POSITION AFTER WHITE'S 10TH MOVE
(G. Lazard v. Znosko-Borovsky, Paris, 1931)

By the same move P—KKt4 Black profits by the direct threats to the White Bishop at KB4 and to the Knight, to open two lines of attack on White's King and to prevent him castling. Without these tactical possibilities, the object of the move, although good in itself, would perhaps not be attained.

Side by side with your strategical intentions chance positions occur, where tactics, appealing to the imagination, allow you to hasten the decision in your favour. Even there you must understand the relation of these tactical possibilities to the strategical conduct of the development, for a slight advantage, momentarily obtained, can produce far-distant repercussions on the solidity of the structure and bring with it the loss of the game.

You will have noticed that many of the variations given in this book end in equality. This does not mean that the game has lost its interest. For, while White, having the advantage of the move, seeks to maintain and even strengthen it, Black starts the game under a slight handicap (the move), and his immediate object should be to obtain equality in order to assume the offensive eventually. Thus when we say that Black has equalised the game, we mean that the game has reached a critical stage when either White or Black may obtain the advantage.

Above all, the contest forces you to be yourself and to develop a sense of position. Do not trust to your memory or learn variations by heart. Learn how to pick out the directive ideas of an opening for yourself, and above all remember that you alone are the creator of your game, and your task starts with the very first move.

May this little book guide you in your perplexities.

ANSWERS TO QUESTIONS

No. 1 (p. 12): After 1. P—K4, P—K4 ; 2. P—Q4, P×P ; 3. Q×P, Kt—QB3 ; 4. Q—K3, Kt—B3 ; 5. P—K5, Kt—KKt5 ; 6. Q—K2 Black continues with 6. .... P—Q3 ; 7. P—KR3, KKt×KP ; 8. P—KB4, Q—R5 ch.

No. 2 (p. 13): After 1. P—K4, P—K4 ; 2. P—Q4, P×P ; 3. Q×P, Kt—QB3 ; 4. Q—K3, Kt—B3 ; 5. Kt—QB3, B—Kt5 ; 6. B—Q2, O—O ; 7. O—O—O, R—K1 ; 8. B—B4, Kt—K4 the continuation might be 9. B—Kt3, P—Q3 ; 10. P—KR3, B—K3 ; activity in both camps without any decisive advantage.

No. 3 (p. 14): After 1. P—K4, P—K4 ; 2. P—Q4, P×P White, if he does not wish to play the Danish Gambit (3. P—QB3), can continue with either 3. Kt—KB3, transposing into the Scotch Gambit, or 3. B—QB4.

No. 4 (p. 18): After 1. P—K4, P—K4 ; 2. Kt—KB3, Kt—QB3 ; 3. P—B3, P—Q4 ; 4. Q—R4, Kt—B3 (Leonhardt's Gambit) ; 5. Kt×P, B—Q3 White can defend himself

by 6. Kt×Kt, P×Kt ; 7. P—Q3, O—O ; 8. B—Kt5, P—KR3 ;
9. B×Kt, Q×B ; 10 Kt—Q2, followed by O—O—O.

No. 5 (p. 23) : After 1. P—K4, P—K4 ; 2. Kt—QB3,
Kt—QB3 ; 3. B—B4, Kt—B3 ; 4. P—Q3, B—Kt5 ; 5. B—
KKt5, P—KR3 ; 6. B×Kt, B×Kt ch ; 7. P×B, Q×B ;
8. Kt—K2, P—Q3 ; 9. O—O, P—KKt4 White replies to
Black's advance on the wing by one in the centre : 10. P—Q4,
P—KR4 ; 11. P—B3, P—R5 ; 12. Q—Q3, B—Q2 ; 13. QR—
Kt1, R—QKt1 ; 14. KR—Q1, etc.

No. 6 (p. 25) : After 1. P—K4, P—K4 ; 2. Kt—KB3,
Kt—KB3 ; 3. B—B4 one can either transpose into the Two
Knights' Defence by 3. .... Kt—B3 or accept the gambit
by 3. .... Kt×P followed by P—Q4, e.g., 3. .... Kt×P ;
4. P—Q3, Kt—B4 ; 5. Kt×P, P—Q4 ; 6. B—Kt3, Kt×B ;
7. RP×Kt, B—Q3 ; 8. P—Q4, O—O, etc.

No. 7 (p. 32) : In Steinitz's combination : 1. P—K4,
P—K4 ; 2. Kt—KB3, Kt—QB3 ; 3. B—B4, B—B4 ; 4. P—
Q3, Kt—B3 ; 5. O—O, P—Q3 ; 6. B—KKt5, P—KR3 ;
7. B—R4, P—KKt4 ; 8. B—KKt3, P—KR4 ; 9. Kt×KtP,
P—R5 ; 10. Kt×P, P×B ; 11. Kt×Q, B—KKt5, ; 12. Q—Q2,
Kt—Q5 White, instead of playing 13. Kt—B3, can, in his
turn, make a Queen sacrifice by playing 13. P—KR3 and so
prolong the struggle.

No. 8 (p. 33) : After 1. P—K4, P—K4 ; 2. Kt—KB3,
Kt—QB3 ; 3. B—B4, B—B4 ; 4. P—B3, Kt—B3 ; 5. P—Q4,
P×P ; 6. P×P, B—Kt5 ch ; 7. B—Q2, B×B ch ; 8. QKt×B,
P—Q4 ; 9. P×P, KKt×P ; 10. Q—Kt3, QKt—K2 ; 11.
O—O, O—O ; 12 KR—K1, P—QB3 White can play 13. Kt—
K4, Kt—QKt3 ; 14 Kt—B5 with the idea of exploiting his
opponent's weakness on the black squares.

No. 9 (p. 34) : After 1. P—K4, P—K4 ; 2. Kt—KB3,
Kt—QB3 ; 3. B—B4, B—B4 ; 4. P—B3, Kt—B3 ; 5. P—Q4,
P×P ; 6. P×P, B—Kt5 ch ; 7. Kt—B3, Kt×KP ; 8. O—O,
B×Kt ; 9. P—Q5 (the Möller Attack), B—B3 ; 10. R—K1,
Kt—K2 ; 11. R×Kt, P—Q3 ; 12. B—Kt5, B×B ; 13. Kt×B,
O—O ; 14. Kt×RP, K×Kt ; 15. Q—R5 ch, K—Kt1 ;
16. R—R4, P—KB4 ; 17. R—K1, Kt—Kt3 ; 18. R—R3,
R—B3 the attack can be continued with 19. R—KKt3,
K—B2 ; 20. R—K6,

No. 10 (p. 37): After 1. P—K4, P—K4 ; 2. Kt—KB3, Kt—QB3 ; 3. B—B4, B—B4 ; 4. P—QKt4, B×P ; 5. P—B3, B—R4 ; 6. P—Q4, P—Q3 ; 7. O—O, B—Kt3 (Lasker's defence to the Evans Gambit) White can regain the pawn —but with the inferior game—by playing 8. P×P, P×P ; 9. Q×Q ch, Kt×Q ; 10. Kt×P, B—K3 or he can play for an attack by 8. P×P, P×P ; 9. Q—Kt3, Q—B3 ; 10. B—KKt5, Q—Kt3 ; 11. B—Q5, etc.

No. 11 (p. 40): After 1. P—K4, P—K4 ; 2. Kt—KB3, Kt—QB3 ; 3. B—B4, Kt—B3 ; 4. P—Q4, P×P ; 5. O—O, B—B4 ; 6. P—K5, P—Q4 ; 7. P×Kt (the Max Lange Attack), P×B ; 8. R—K1 ch, B—K3 ; 9. Kt—Kt5, Q—Q4 ; 10. Kt—QB3, Q—B4; 11. QKt—K4, O—O—O; 12. KKt×B, P×Kt ; 13. P—KKt4, Q—K4 ; 14. P×P, KR—Kt1 ; 15. B—R6, P—Q6 ; 16. P—QB3 Black can play 16. .... P—Q7 ; 17. R—K2, B—Kt3 with a faint chance of equalising the game.

No. 12 (p. 40): After 1. P—K4, P—K4 ; 2. Kt—KB3, Kt—QB3 ; 3. B—B4, Kt—B3 (the Two Knights' Defence) ; 4. P—Q4, P×P ; 5. O—O, Kt×P ; 6. R—K1, P—Q4 ; 7. B×P, Q×B ; 8. Kt—B3, Q—Q1 ; 9. R×Kt ch, B—K2 ; 10. Kt×P, P—B4 ; 11. R—B4, O—O White's King's Rook should play an active role and attack Black's weakened pawns : 12. Kt×Kt, Q×Q ch ; 13. Kt×Q, P×Kt, but on the fourth rank it will be subjected to repeated attacks by the hostile Bishops, therefore White will do best to retreat it to the third rank and so open a diagonal for his Bishop.

No. 13 (p. 41): After 1. P—K4, P—K4 ; 2. Kt—KB3, Kt—QB3 ; 3. B—B4, Kt—B3 ; 4. Kt—Kt5, P—Q4 ; 5. P×P, Kt×P ; 6. Kt×BP, K×Kt ; 7. Q—B3 ch, K—K3 ; 8. Kt—B3, Kt—Kt5 White continues the attack with 9. Q—K4, P—B3 ; 10. P—QR3, Kt—R3 ; 11. P—Q4, etc. I give here a game played at this variation (White : Znosko-Borovsky) : 9. O—O, P—B3 ; 10. P—Q4, Kt×BP ; 11. P×P, Kt×R ; 12. R—Q1, Kt—B7 ; 13. Kt×Kt, P×Kt ; 14. B×P ch, Q×B ; 15. Q×Q ch, K—K2 ; 16. B—Kt5 ch, K—K1 ; 17. P—K6, B—K2 ; 18. Q—Q8 ch, B×Q ; 19. R×B mate.

No. 14 (p. 41): After 1. P—K4, P—K4 ; 2. Kt—KB3, Kt—QB3 ; 3. B—B4, Kt—B3 ; 4. Kt—Kt5, P—Q4 ; 5. P×P, Kt—QR4 ; 6. B—Kt5 ch, P—B3 ; 7. P×P, P×P ; 8. B—K2,

P—KR3 ; 9. Kt—KB3, P—K5 ; 10. Kt—K5, B—Q3 ;
11. P—Q4, Q—B2 ; 12. P—KB4, Black continues with
12. .... P×P *e.p.* ; 13. Kt×P (B3), Kt—Kt5.

No. 15 (p. 44): After 1. P—K4, P—K4 ; 2. Kt—KB3,
Kt—QB3 ; 3. B—Kt5, B—B4 (the Classical Defence to the
Ruy Lopez) White should exploit the position of the Bishop
at Black's QB4 and play 4. P—B3. Black then has the
choice between the quiet move 4. .... B—Kt3 and the
attack 4. .... P—B4.

No. 16 (p. 53): After 1. P—K4, P—K4 ; 2. Kt—KB3,
Kt—QB3 ; 3. B—Kt5, P—Q3 ; 4. P—Q4, Kt—B3 ; 5. O—O,
B—Q2 ; 6. R—K1, B—K2 ; 7. Kt—B3 (Tarrasch's trap),
O—O ; 8. B×Kt, B×B ; 9. P×P, P×P ; 10. Q×Q, B×Q,
White simply gains the pawn by 12. Kt×P.

No. 17 (p. 55): After 1. P—K4, P—K4 ; 2. Kt—KB3,
Kt—QB3 ; 3. B—Kt5, P—QR3 ; 4. B—R4, P—Q3 ; 5. P—B3,
P—B4 (the Siesta Gambit) ; 6. P×P, B×P ; 7. P—Q4,
P—K5 ; 8. Kt—Kt5 Black can play (instead of 8. ....
Kt—B3) 8. .... P—Q4, since the continuation 9. P—B3,
P—K6 ; 10. B×P, P—R3 ; 11. Kt—KR3, B×Kt gives
White no advantage.

No. 18 (p. 56): After 1. P—K4, P—K4 ; 2. Kt—KB3,
Kt—QB3 ; 3. Kt—B3, Kt—B3 (the Four Knights' Game) ; 4.
B—Kt5, B—Kt5 ; 5. O—O, O—O ; 6. P—Q3, B×Kt ; 7. P×B,
P—Q4 ; 8. B×Kt, P×B ; 9. Kt×P, Q—Q3 ; 10. B—B4,
R—K1 ; 11. Q—B3, P×P ; 12. P×P, R×Kt, White should
play 13. QR—Q1, B—Kt5 ; 14. R×Q (if 14. Q—Kt3, then
14. .... Kt×P), B×Q ; 15. R×Kt, etc., and *not* 13. KR—Q1,
to which Black would reply with 13. .... B—Kt5 ; 14.
Q—Kt3, B×R ; 15. B×R, Q—Q7, threatening Q—K8 mate.
A very deep trap !

No. 19 (p. 57): After 1. P—K4, P—K4 ; 2. Kt—KB3,
Kt—QB3 ; 3. Kt—B3, Kt—B3 ; 4. B—Kt5, Kt—Q5 (Rubin-
stein's Attack in the Four Knights' Game) ; 5. Kt×P,
Kt×KP ; 6. Kt×Kt, Kt×B ; 7. Kt×BP, Q—K2 ; 8. Kt×R,
Q×Kt ch ; 9. K—B1, Kt—Q5 ; 10. P—Q3, White has the
better game since he will complete his development before
Black captures the Knight, *e.g.*, 10. .... Q—B4 ; 11. P—KR4,
P—QKt3 ; 12. B—Kt5, P—Kt3 ; 13. Q—Q2, B—KKt2 ;
14. R—K1 ch, etc.

The following continuation is more difficult for White :
5. .... Q—K2 ; 6. P—B4, Kt×B ; 7. Kt×Kt, P—Q3 ;
8. Kt—KB3, Q×P ch ; 9. K—B2, Kt—Kt5 ch ; 10. K—Kt3,
Q—Kt3 ; 11. Kt—R4, Q—R4 ; 12. P—KR3 (if 12. Kt×BP ch,
then 12. .... K—Q1 ; 13. Kt×R, P—KKt4), Q×Kt ;
13. P×Kt. Black has two Bishops and a compact pawn
formation, moreover White's King is not in a safe position.

No. 20 (p. 61) : After 1. P—K4, P—K4 ; 2. P—KB4,
B—B4 (the King's Gambit Declined) ; 3. Kt—KB3, P—Q3 ;
4. P—B3, B—Kt3 ; 5. P×P, P×P ; 6. Kt×P, Black continues with 6. .... Q—R5 ch ; 7. P—Kt3, Q×KP ch.

No. 21 (p. 63) : After 1. P—K4, P—K4 ; 2. P—KB4,
P—Q4 (the Falkbeer Counter-Gambit) ; 3. KP×P, P—QB3,
White cannot play 4. QP×P, Kt×P ; 5. P×P because of
5. .... Q—R5 ch followed by 6. .... Q—K5 ch.

No. 22 (p. 66) : 1. P—K4, P—K4 ; 2. P—KB4, P×P ;
3. B—B4, Q—R5 ch ; 4. K—B1, P—KKt4 ; 5. Kt—QB3,
B—Kt2 ; 6. P—Q4, Kt—K2, etc.

No. 23 (p. 83) : After 1. P—Q4, P—Q4 ; 2. P—QB4,
P—K4 ; 3. QP×P, P—Q5 ; 4. P—K3, B—Kt5 ch ; 5. B—Q2,
P×P ; 6. B×B, P×P ch ; 7. K—K2, P×Kt(=Kt) ch, the
continuation would be 8. K—K1 (if 8. R×Kt, then 8. ....
B—Kt5 ch), Q—R5 ch ; 9. K—Q2 (if 9. P—Kt3, then 9. ....
Q—K5 ch), Q—B7 ch ; 10. K—B1, B—Kt5, etc.

No. 24 (p. 85) : After 1. P—Q4, P—Q4 ; 2. P—QB4,
P—K3 ; 3. Kt—QB3, Kt—KB3 ; 4. B—Kt5, B—K2 ;
5. P—K3, QKt—Q2 ; 6. Kt—B3, O—O ; 7. R—B1, P—B3 ;
8. B—Q3, P×P ; 9. B×P, Kt—Q4 ; 10. B×B, Q×B ;
11. O—O, Kt×Kt ; 12. R×Kt, P—K4 ; 13. P×P, Kt×P ;
14. Kt×Kt, Q×Kt ; 15. P—B4, the best move is 15. ....
Q—K5, fixing, at any rate temporarily, the pawn at K3.
If, instead, 15. .... Q—B3, then 16. P—K4, or, if 15. ....
Q—K2, then 16. P—B5.

No. 25 (p. 88) : If, after 1. P—Q4, P—Q4 ; 2. P—QB4,
P—K3 ; 3. Kt—QB3, P—QB4 ; 4. BP×P, KP×P ; 5. Kt—B3,
Kt—QB3 ; 6. P—KKt3, Kt—B3 ; 7. B—Kt2, B—K2 ;
8. O—O, O—O ; 9. P×P, B×P, White plays 10. B—Kt5,
then 10. .... P—Q5 ; 11. Kt—K4, B—K2.

If White plays B—Kt5 at his 9th move (instead of 9. P×P), then 9. .... B—K3 ; 10. P×P, B×P ; 11. R—B1, B—Kt3, etc.

No. 26 (p. 90) : After 1. P—Q4, P—Q4 ; 2. P—QB4, P—QB3 ; 3. Kt—KB3, Kt—B3 ; 4. Kt—B3, P×P ; 5. P—QR4, P—K3, White plays 6. P—K4, B—Kt5 ; 7. P—K5, Kt—Q4 ; 8. B—Q2.

If 5. .... B—B4 (instead of 5. .... P—K3) ; 6. Kt—K5, P—K3, then 7. B—Kt5 or first 7. P—B3 and (after 7. .... B—QKt5) 8. B—Kt5 but *not* 8. P—K4, which would lead to the following interesting combination : 8. .... B×P ; 9. P×B, Kt×P ; 10. Q—B3, Q×P, etc.

No. 27 (p. 92) : After 1. P—Q4, P—Q4 ; 2. P—QB4, P—K3 ; 3. Kt—QB3, Kt—KB3 ; 4. B—Kt5, QKt—Q2 ; 5. P—K3, P—B3 ; 6. Kt—B3, Q—R4 ; 7. Kt—Q2, B—Kt5 ; 8. Q—B2, O—O, the move 9. B—Q3 would lose a piece on account of the reply 9. .... P×P. We see here the realisation of the threat of the Queen on White's Queen's Bishop.

No. 28 (p. 105) : After 1. P—K4, P—K3 ; 2. P—Q4, P—Q4 ; 3. Kt—QB3, Kt—KB3 ; 4. B—Kt5, B—Kt5 ; 5. P—K5, P—KR3 ; 6. B—R4, the continuation might be 6. .... P—KKt4 ; 7. B—Kt3, Kt—K5 ; 8. Kt—K2, P—QB4 ; 9. P—QR3, etc.

No 29 (p. 106) : After 1. P—K4, P—K3 ; 2. P—Q4, P—Q4 ; 3. Kt—QB3, Kt—KB3 ; 4. B—Kt5, B—K2 ; 5. P—K5, KKt—Q2 ; 6. B×B, Q×B ; 7. Kt—Kt5, Black defends himself by 7. .... Q—Q1 ; 8. P—QB3, P—QR3 ; 9. Kt—QR3, P—QB4 ; 10. P—KB4, Kt—QB3 ; 11. Kt—B3, arriving at a position just as typical as that mentioned on p. 105, with an interesting game with Knights and pawns on the Queen's wing.

No. 30 (p. 108) : After 1. P—K4, P—QB3 ; 2. P—Q4, P—Q4 ; 3. P×P, P×P ; 4. P—QB4, Kt—KB3 ; 5. Kt—QB3, Kt—B3 ; 6. Kt—B3, B—Kt5 ; 7. P×P, KKt×P ; 8. B—QKt5, Black should play 8. .... R—B1 and *not* 8. .... Q—R4 ; 9. Q—Kt3, B×Kt ; 10. P×B, Kt×Kt ; 11. P×Kt.

No. 31 (p. 108) : After 1. P—K4, P—QB3 ; 2. P—Q4, P—Q4 ; 3. Kt—QB3, P×P ; 4. Kt×P, B—B4 ; 5. Kt—Kt3,

B—Kt3 ; 6. P—KR4, P—KR3, White plays 7. Kt—B3, Kt—Q2 ; 8. P—R5, B—R2 ; 9. B—Q3, B×B ; 10. Q×B, KKt—B3 ; 11. B—Q2 to prevent Q—R4 and to play O—O—O as soon as possible. (This variation can also be played without the moves 8. P—R5 and 8. .... B—R2).

No. 32 (p. 111): After 1. P—K4, P—QB4 ; 2. P—QB4 Black can either (1) bring about a symmetrical position by 2. .... P—K4 or (2) exploit the weakness of White's Q4 by playing 2. .... Kt—QB3 or (3) prepare to make the advance P—Q4.

No. 33 (p. 111): After 1. P—K4, P—QB4 ; 2. Kt—QB3 Black can either open the centre by P—K3 and P—Q4 or form a backward centre by imitating White's moves, *e.g.*, 2. .... Kt—QB3 ; 3. P—KKt3, P—KKt3 ; 4. B—Kt2, B—Kt2 ; 5. P—Q3, P—Q3 ; 6. KKt—K2, etc.

No. 34 (p. 132): In Nimzowitsch's variation the Bishop at QKt5 cannot be captured by the Queen because of the reply Kt—B7 ch.

No. 35 (p. 133): The Queen's Fianchetto variation by Black reminds us of the Sicilian Defence.

No. 36 (p. 136): Réti's Gambit (1. Kt—KB3, P—Q4 ; 2. P—B4) may be declined by 2. .... P—K3 or 2. .... P—QB3. 2. .... P—Q5 would be bad because after 3. P—QKt4 and 4. P—K3 Black's Queen's pawn would become weak.

A CATALOGUE OF SELECTED DOVER BOOKS
IN ALL FIELDS OF INTEREST

A CATALOGUE OF SELECTED DOVER
BOOKS IN ALL FIELDS OF INTEREST

RACKHAM'S COLOR ILLUSTRATIONS FOR WAGNER'S RING. Rackham's finest mature work—all 64 full-color watercolors in a faithful and lush interpretation of the *Ring*. Full-sized plates on coated stock of the paintings used by opera companies for authentic staging of Wagner. Captions aid in following complete Ring cycle. Introduction. 64 illustrations plus vignettes. 72pp. 8⅝ x 11¼. 23779-6 Pa. $6.00

CONTEMPORARY POLISH POSTERS IN FULL COLOR, edited by Joseph Czestochowski. 46 full-color examples of brilliant school of Polish graphic design, selected from world's first museum (near Warsaw) dedicated to poster art. Posters on circuses, films, plays, concerts all show cosmopolitan influences, free imagination. Introduction. 48pp. 9⅜ x 12¼. 23780-X Pa. $6.00

GRAPHIC WORKS OF EDVARD MUNCH, Edvard Munch. 90 haunting, evocative prints by first major Expressionist artist and one of the greatest graphic artists of his time: *The Scream, Anxiety, Death Chamber, The Kiss, Madonna*, etc. Introduction by Alfred Werner. 90pp. 9 x 12. 23765-6 Pa. $5.00

THE GOLDEN AGE OF THE POSTER, Hayward and Blanche Cirker. 70 extraordinary posters in full colors, from Maitres de l'Affiche, Mucha, Lautrec, Bradley, Cheret, Beardsley, many others. Total of 78pp. 9⅜ x 12¼. 22753-7 Pa. $5.95

THE NOTEBOOKS OF LEONARDO DA VINCI, edited by J. P. Richter. Extracts from manuscripts reveal great genius; on painting, sculpture, anatomy, sciences, geography, etc. Both Italian and English. 186 ms. pages reproduced, plus 500 additional drawings, including studies for *Last Supper*, Sforza monument, etc. 860pp. 7⅞ x 10¾. (Available in U.S. only) 22572-0, 22573-9 Pa., Two-vol. set $15.90

THE CODEX NUTTALL, as first edited by Zelia Nuttall. Only inexpensive edition, in full color, of a pre-Columbian Mexican (Mixtec) book. 88 color plates show kings, gods, heroes, temples, sacrifices. New explanatory, historical introduction by Arthur G. Miller. 96pp. 11⅜ x 8½. (Available in U.S. only) 23168-2 Pa. $7.95

UNE SEMAINE DE BONTÉ, A SURREALISTIC NOVEL IN COLLAGE, Max Ernst. Masterpiece created out of 19th-century periodical illustrations, explores worlds of terror and surprise. Some consider this Ernst's greatest work. 208pp. 8⅛ x 11. 23252-2 Pa. $6.00

GEOMETRY, RELATIVITY AND THE FOURTH DIMENSION, Rudolf Rucker. Exposition of fourth dimension, means of visualization, concepts of relativity as Flatland characters continue adventures. Popular, easily followed yet accurate, profound. 141 illustrations. 133pp. 5⅜ x 8½.
23400-2 Pa. $2.75

THE ORIGIN OF LIFE, A. I. Oparin. Modern classic in biochemistry, the first rigorous examination of possible evolution of life from nitrocarbon compounds. Non-technical, easily followed. Total of 295pp. 5⅜ x 8½.
60213-3 Pa. $4.00

PLANETS, STARS AND GALAXIES, A. E. Fanning. Comprehensive introductory survey: the sun, solar system, stars, galaxies, universe, cosmology; quasars, radio stars, etc. 24pp. of photographs. 189pp. 5⅜ x 8½. (Available in U.S. only)
21680-2 Pa. $3.75

THE THIRTEEN BOOKS OF EUCLID'S ELEMENTS, translated with introduction and commentary by Sir Thomas L. Heath. Definitive edition. Textual and linguistic notes, mathematical analysis, 2500 years of critical commentary. Do not confuse with abridged school editions. Total of 1414pp. 5⅜ x 8½.   60088-2, 60089-0, 60090-4 Pa., Three-vol. set $18.50

Prices subject to change without notice.

Available at your book dealer or write for free catalogue to Dept. GI, Dover Publications, Inc., 180 Varick St., N.Y., N.Y. 10014. Dover publishes more than 175 books each year on science, elementary and advanced mathematics, biology, music, art, literary history, social sciences and other areas.